# Can You Spare a Minute?

Zu Vorträgen bildnisse

# Can You Spare a Minute?

Roy Williamson

*Foreword by George Carey*

**daybreak**
London

First published in 1991 by
Daybreak
Darton, Longman and Todd Ltd
89 Lillie Road, London SW6 1UD

Reprinted 1991

ISBN 0–232–51922–6

A catalogue record of this book
is available from the British Library

Unless otherwise stated
the scriptural quotations are taken from the New Jerusalem Bible
published and copyright 1985 by
Darton, Longman and Todd Ltd and Doubleday and Co Inc.,
and used by permission of the publishers

Phototypeset by Intype, London
Printed and bound in Great Britain by
Courier International Ltd, East Kilbride, Scotland

To

ANNE

who has spared me
more minutes than
I can ever repay

# Contents

# Contents

# Foreword

I first met Roy when he was vicar of a tough inner city church in Nottingham and I was lecturer in theology at St John's Theological College. Our friendship grew out of close contact as we tried to help students relate to the needs and challenges of inner city ministry. I soon discovered Roy's remarkable flair to reach people with his ready Irish wit, his preaching ability and his genuine interest in people. But I also realised that these gifts and many others I could mention were secondary to his love for Christ and his desire to proclaim 'good news' about him.

And that is what this book is about. Not about Roy Williamson or about Church life but about faith, hope and other important things that really matter. *Can You Spare a Minute?* is a readable and sensitive book that actually starts where people are with their questions, doubts and fears. Its very simplicity is its appeal and Roy shows his ability as a communicator to say things in such a way that people unlearned in 'churchy' things can understand.

Roy says at the end of his Introduction that 'If I have a motive for writing such a book, it is the gospel of Jesus. I am still excited and enthralled by God's *Good News*'.

That enthusiasm comes shining through and it is my hope that Roy's book will be a useful tool for the Decade of Evangelism.

✝ George Cantuar

# Introduction

Two incidents came to mind as I responded to an invitation to write this little book. The first is humorous. The second is deadly serious. Both are very pertinent to the task I set myself in the pages which follow.

The first took place when I was a vicar. The evening service had ended and I was shaking hands with a very large number of people who were leaving the church. One rather vivacious lady made a bee-line for me, gave me a huge grin, shook me warmly by the hand and with great enthusiasm said, 'Roy, I get a marvellous feeling when I see you climbing the pulpit steps. I love it when you preach.' Sinner that I am I encouraged her to enlarge a little on such sentiments – when it comes to flattery, all donations are gratefully received – what had I said to produce such devotion? 'Oh!' she replied, somewhat surprised. 'It's nothing that you say. It's the way you take your watch off and place it on the pulpit before you begin!'

That little incident still causes me to laugh. It still helps me not to take myself too seriously. It still serves to dispel the illusion that a captive audience, with a polite, intelligent expression on all faces is hanging on my every word. Above all it continues to teach me that communication does not necessarily occur because I am speaking and other people appear to be listening. There's more to it than that.

The second incident took place soon after I became a bishop. Again I had been preaching and after the service a teenager, with the bluntness for which Yorkshire is famous, said to me, 'Sir, was that true – or was it preaching?' It was a very painful and perceptive comment. It wasn't just that I had said something which had helped and inspired him. It was the challenging distinction he made between what was true and what was merely 'preaching'. As I chatted with that young man it became apparent that the real distinction he was wishing to make was between theory and practice. Between words, however beautifully expressed, and the everyday experiences of life. Unless what he heard from the preacher made genuine connections with what he knew to be true of life it remained in the realm of 'preaching' rather than reality.

Both of these incidents made a great impression on me. They reminded me of the many on the fringes of church life – or even within the church – who simply are not hearing the things we are trying to say. And if they do hear them apparently they bear little relevance to their everyday life.

So this book is my humble effort to teach basic Christian truth to those who find it difficult to grasp and to root in ordinary life. I have in mind those who may not have the inclination to read a specifically 'theological' book. I take little for granted except a very limited knowledge of Christian truth and I try to build upon it in such a way as to encourage rather than exclude the reader. Because of my own personal experience I tend to view the reader as someone who is already on the Christian journey – even though they may not yet have realised it – and try to offer help along the way.

I have tried to address some of the major and fundamental doctrines of the Christian Church in language which I hope people will understand. In order to do this I have included images and stories from everyday life and used them as starting-points for communicating the kind of truth which I consider vital for the development of the life of faith.

Busy people will not want to spend time and effort reading through endless pages of sustained argument, nor will they wish to be directed elsewhere in order to pursue a line of thought. Bearing this in mind I try to present glimpses of truth, hopefully in palatable form and in manageable portions. In this connection the title gives the clue. *Can You Spare a Minute?* is meant to signal to the reader that it is not going to take her or him an age to 'get to the point' of the particular truth in question. The text reinforces this message by being presented in sections which can be read within a minute or two.

If I have a motive for writing such a book it is the gospel of Jesus. I am still excited and enthralled by God's *Good News*. Imaginatively presented I believe it can warm the heart, inspire the mind and transform the life. If my humble effort fails to do this the fault is mine – it is certainly not the fault of the gospel.

# 1

## The Way In
### *Prayer – a primary approach to God*

Earlier that afternoon I had been rushed into hospital. The diagnosis was 'a stone in the kidney'. So I lay in bed feeling sorry for myself, suffering the agony that accompanies such a condition and not at all encouraged by the 'words of comfort' from the man in the next bed. 'It will get worse before it gets better', he assured me. Isn't it marvellous how some people always seem to have just the right word for every occasion!

Unfortunately he was right and as the afternoon progressed the pain increased. When my discomfort was at its worst I had two visitors: the Anglican chaplain and the local Baptist pastor. I can vaguely recall them standing like book-ends on either side of my bed looking suitably concerned and revealing all the signs of helplessness. After a brief period, during which they made sympathetic noises in my direction, they decided to have a conversation with each other. It went something like this: 'I think we ought to say a prayer for him, don't you?' said the Anglican. 'I agree', replied the Baptist. Heavens, I thought, things must be bad. 'Since you are the chaplain,' said the local pastor, 'I think you ought to say the prayer, after all I am only a Baptist pastor.' 'Oh, that's all right', retorted the Anglican chaplain magnanimously, 'I've never heard a Baptist pastor pray before, so I think it would be nice if you said the prayer.'

At that point my patience deserted me and my irritation, fuelled by my pain, asserted itself. 'It was good of you to come, fellas,' I said, 'now push off and I'll pray for myself.'


## PRAYER — THE WAY IN . . .

That incident, while it highlights several issues, focuses the attention on a basic fact of life, namely, that a great many people, perhaps the majority, feel that prayer to God in the face of helplessness and need is the only, indeed the most important, thing they can do. They may or may not be religious. They may be unable to articulate any particular faith or creed. They may not even be fully convinced that there is a God. But if there is they seem reasonably confident that 'the way in' to God is through prayer.

I find this basic fact being reinforced every day of my life. The most unlikely people in the most unlikely places reveal that prayer plays a part, however small, in their life. Of course they won't talk about it openly, for after all it's not the done thing for the average English person to go public about his or her religion. Nevertheless a remarkably large number of people consider themselves to be within easy reach of God. Not in any committed nor over-emotional sense, but through their occasional prayers. Indeed, it is a salutary fact for those of us who are church leaders to consider, that many who have little or no time for church-going are in no doubt about the possibility of 'getting in touch with God' – and the way in is the way of prayer.

## IN TROUBLE . . .

Early in my life as a bishop I was involved in an experience that will remain with me for the rest of my life. It was the Bradford Fire Disaster of 1985. What had begun as a day of great celebration – Bradford City had just won promotion to the Second Division of the Football League – ended in tragedy as fifty-six people died in the horrendous fire which swept with speed and ferocity through the main stand. The match was being televised and so millions throughout the nation witnessed the horror of the disaster as it happened. The entire community of Bradford was devastated by the tragedy and numbed by the shock – though it needs to be said that the response of the statutory and voluntary services, together with that of a vast number of unnamed individuals, was magnificent.

The Provost of Bradford Cathedral and I had an urgent conversation quite late on the Saturday the tragedy occurred. We sensed the need of the people of Bradford to express their solidarity in sympathy and sorrow with all those who had suffered. We felt it right to offer an opportunity for people to come together for prayer in the cathedral the next day. The only publicity possible at that late stage was an announcement on local radio on Sunday morning. There was an amazing response. A cathedral full to overflowing with hundreds standing inside and several more hundreds standing outside during the thirty-minute service of prayer.

It was an incredible testimony to people's need, in the face of inexplicable disaster and suffering, to be in touch with God – either to weep in sorrow or shake their fist in anger – and prayer was the way in. The huge crowd in Bradford Cathedral that Sunday afternoon was but a symbol of a whole community 'praying' to God, whoever their God was, in a time of helplessness and need.

AND IN JOY . . .

A lifetime spent working with people, both inside and outside the Church, leads me to the conviction that it is not only in times of personal and corporate tragedy that people pray. There is a similar, if less dramatic, response at times of great personal and community experiences of thanksgiving and celebration. National joy on grand and significant occasions is normally expressed not only in pomp and circumstance but also in services of prayer and thanksgiving to God. While at the personal level those great pivotal points of human existence, birth, marriage and death are, more often than not, accompanied by prayer to God.

I can remember, as though it were yesterday, being interrupted while planting some seedlings in one of my churchyards in the early days of my ministry as a local vicar. A young man whom I had never seen before approached and entered the church door. Now I know that vicars are supposed to be 'other-worldly' but they are also sinners. So as he emerged from the church door after ten minutes I mentally frisked him – examining the contour of his clothes for any tell-tale signs that he was borrowing the church silver. To my shame but also to my delight he came and asked me where the vicar lived – I was well disguised in gardening clothes. When I revealed my identity he inarticulately but very sincerely told me of the birth of his first child the night before. No, he hadn't come to ask if the vicar would baptise his baby. He had come to church so that he could pray to God and give thanks for the birth of his new son. Now he was wanting to find the vicar to donate to the church a tangible expression of his gratitude. It is just worth recording that that man and his family became sincere followers of the

4

Christian way. Prayer in response to personal joy became a 'way in' to God.

Prayer has been described as 'the Christian's vital breath' but I believe it is also part of the experience of men and women in every walk of life. Their grasp on Christian truth may be tenuous and their relationship to the church may be tentative. But they pray, if only occasionally, and they believe that their prayer carries them into the presence of God.

RELATIONSHIP . . .

If prayer, in some shape or form, is part of the universal human experience, ought we to be content with the occasional dash into the presence of God at times of sorrow or joy? Is God happy with this kind of periodic prayer or does he get upset that we are simply using him for our own selfish ends? Has he given us any clues of a more satisfactory and fulfilling way of going on that may bring enrichment to the whole of our lives? I believe he has.

One of my favourite New Testament stories is of the woman who touched the hem of our Lord's garment in order to be healed of her disease.

Now there was a woman who had suffered from a haemorrhage for twelve years; after long and painful treatment under various doctors, she had spent all she had without being any the better for it; in fact, she was getting worse. She had heard about Jesus, and she came up through the crowd and touched his cloak from behind, thinking, 'If I can just touch his clothes, I shall be saved.' And at once the source of the bleeding dried up, and she felt in herself that she was cured of her complaint. And at once aware of the power that had gone out of him, Jesus turned round in the crowd and said, 'Who touched my clothes?' His disciples said to him, 'You see how the crowd is pressing round you; how can you ask, "Who touched me?" ' But he continued to look all round to see who had done it. Then the woman came forward, frightened and trembling because she knew what had happened to her, and she fell at his feet and told him the whole truth. 'My daughter,' he said, 'your faith has restored you to health; go in peace and be free of your complaint.'

Mark 5:25–34

The fascinating part of this story for me is that this unnamed woman, determined to remain a private person, approaches Jesus within the anonymity of the crowd; expresses her silent prayer for healing by way of an outstretched hand – and is healed on her own terms. The healing power of Jesus flowed from him even before he knew who had touched him. But the important thing is he wasn't willing to leave it at that. To have done so could have left the woman with a somewhat miraculous view of cloth. Instead Jesus provoked a personal encounter with her and transformed what might have been a mere mechanical act into a personal relationship. For twelve years she had watched doctor after doctor shake their heads before her. She had watched society withdraw from her. She had seen the church close its doors against her. But what she found in Jesus was acceptance, assurance and peace based on relationship.

The incredible goodness of God as reflected in Jesus enables him to be gracious in response to our selfishness. If God waited until our motives for praying were pure it is doubtful if we would have any of our prayers answered. His love, generosity and compassion are without strings.

6

Nevertheless there are clear indications that the most satisfying experience of prayer either leads to or springs from a meaningful relationship between God and the one who prays. Indeed, as far as I am concerned, relationship is the key word. At its simplest and, perhaps, at its most profound prayer *is* relationship. Certainly that was the reality which formed the basis of the prayers and of the life of Jesus. One word above all others revealed what prayer meant to him. It was the word *abba* or Father. It dominated his prayers at the great pivotal points of his life and it demonstrated that they sprang from an intimate relationship with his heavenly Father.

INTO PERSPECTIVE . . .

It is this idea of relationship which helps to put some of the more 'unacceptable' aspects of prayer into perspective.

I am sure that my teenagers were neither more subtle nor more sinful than anyone else's but I have a clear and interesting recollection of them during their late teenage years. On certain occasions the natural truculence of youth was replaced miraculously with a ready cooperation that defied belief – but it was usually a precursor to asking if they might borrow their dad's car! 'I'll scratch your back if you'll scratch mine' may not be a very enlightened approach to prayer to God – though there are traces of it in the Bible – but it loses its superficial offensiveness in the relationship that makes for prayer. The thinly disguised subtleness of my teenagers didn't stop me from lending them the car.

We don't really have to try to twist God's arm to ensure that we get what we want. If a relationship based on love exists between us prayer becomes more of an adventure rather than a battle of wills – or wits. A way of life rather

7

than an occasional experience. Indeed that is how I have always viewed the Lord's Prayer. Not so much a prayer – more a way of life.

OPEN TO GOD . . .

Prayer, properly understood, can be seen as the opening of our whole life to God.

Like so many other aspects of the Christian life there is a paradox here. In one sense we don't need to open our lives to God for they are already open to him. As Paul reminded the Christians at Rome, 'To God our lives lie open'. The cynic in me recalls many prayer meetings when those present, myself included, seemed to suffer from the illusion that the Almighty was not only blind and hard of hearing, but that he was also seriously disadvantaged by not having a television, radio or morning paper – and so we proceeded to tell him what was happening in his world. Oh how easy it is to equate prayer with words and to rush headlong into the presence of God with well-meaning but unnecessary verbiage.

Of course God knows our thoughts before we express them and, of course, we can't tell God anything he doesn't know already. But it would be wrong to deduce from this that prayer, therefore, is pointless. One of the most pertinent little questions I ever heard was, 'Does God steam open his children's letters?' In other words does he treat us as children or trust us as adults? There is much in the Bible to remind us that the latter is the case – especially regarding prayer. 'What do you want me to do for you?' Jesus asked blind Bartimaeus when the latter sought his help on the Jericho road (Mark 10:51). Everyone else assumed that no consultation was needed and that Jesus would 'do the necessary' and give Bartimaeus back his sight. But Jesus refused to be paternalistic. He did Bartimaeus the courtesy of allowing him to decide how he could best be helped.

It was St Augustine with his wonderful insight into the ways of God who said, 'God asks our leave to bless us.' In other words he affords us the dignity and gives us the privilege of speaking to him in prayer. Far from treating us as children 'who should be seen and not heard', he · trusts us as adults and invites us to talk to him about the things which may be on our minds.

It is a staggering thought that the Creator of the universe actually encourages his creatures to share with him in this way. But throughout the whole of my Christian life it is those moments spent alone with God in prayer that have proved to be the most vital and enriching. Consciously to open my life to God in this way has been an enormous source of both comfort and challenge. The cynic may say that I, and others like me, have been engaged in a kind of internal therapy – 'talking to myself'. I would not deny that there is an element of therapy about it, for to be in touch with one's Creator in this way has great healing possibilities. But my experience over many years leads me to the firm conviction that, far from talking to myself, I am in communion with one who is prepared to enter into a personal relationship with me. Not only hearing and answering my prayers but, at times, pressing in upon me with challenges to my way of life.

SILENCE IS GOLDEN . . .

But it would be a great mistake to give the impression that prayer must always be linked with words and with speech. It is an even greater mistake to believe that special words – and sometimes a special tone – must be used if we are to make connections with God. This can lead some people to take on a different personality when they pray – so that at times God must wonder who it is that is talking to him.

But prayer is not about words. It is about recognising that we are always in the presence of our Creator and sometimes, indeed more often than not, silence is the only appropriate response. Mind you, silence is not always easily achieved nor, to be honest, is it frequently desired. Silence can be a terrifying thing because it confronts us with ourselves. Metropolitan Anthony Bloom, the Russian archbishop in London, tells the story of a lady who said to him, 'I have prayed all my life, but never really met God.' He advised her, 'Sit still for twenty minutes and whatever you do don't pray.' So she sat down and found that she had time to relax. She began to look at the room, to notice its shapes and colours, to hear the ticking of the clock. The silence grew profound. Then, at the heart of the silence, she became aware of a 'Presence'.

It was Bishop Stephen Verney who wrote, 'Silence can transform prayer so that it is seen not as me trying to attract God's attention, but God trying to attract mine. Not my running to him, but his running to me – as the Father ran to meet the Prodigal Son.' It is good to be still, to be silent, to become aware of God in the heart of the present moment. God coming to me out of creation, out of the Scriptures, out of the sacraments, out of other people.

One of the best known verses from the Psalms is, 'Be still and acknowledge that I am God'. It is important to remember that within their context these words were not meant to be words of comfort for the harassed. On the contrary they were words of rebuke to a restless and turbulent world. Rather like the command of Jesus to the raging sea, 'Peace, be still'. This will give great encouragement to the many whose lives are of necessity filled with activity and pressure. God is not unaware of their situation. He is able to speak a word of peace and reassurance to those in the midst of pressures. It is rarely possible for such people to find a quiet church to slip into for a period of silence. But the daily practice of a brief period of silence and stillness – it may only be five minutes – can become a practical possibility in the midst of the most pressurised life. It is crucial for the balance of all aspects of life. Not only will our relationship with God be enriched, but our mental and physical powers will be the better for it.

## IT DOESN'T ALL DEPEND ON ME . . .

There are times when the subject of prayer depresses me. I listen to talks on prayer from 'experts' and I say to myself, 'Help, I can never match up to that standard.' I go into Christian bookshops and am visually assaulted with books about how to pray and how to pray successfully. On such occasions I have to confess a great temptation to ask for the omnibus edition of *Andy Capp* in order to remind myself of the real world in which I live. Prayer is a serious business, of course, but if I take myself too seriously in connection with it I can quickly develop an unhealthy intensity. This can leave me feeling guilty if I haven't found the time to pray as I should – or as I have been led to believe I should. It can also leave me with a kind of 'holy glow' of self-satisfaction if I have managed to 'say my prayers' properly. When either of these things begin to happen I believe that the danger signals are flashing. Prayer has ceased to be what God intended it to be and has become a vehicle for gaining merit.

The truth of the matter is that it doesn't all depend on me. It was Mother Theresa who said, 'In reality, there is only one true prayer, only one substantial prayer: Christ himself. There is only one voice which rises above the face of the earth: the voice of Christ. His voice unites and co-ordinates in itself all the voices raised in prayer.' The tremendously helpful thing about these words, which have a base in Scripture, is that they can take all the selfish anxiety out of prayer. It really doesn't all depend on me and my skill and experience in prayer – or, for that matter, my lack of them. We do not originate prayer. We simply join in it.

In my lighter moments I have reflected upon silly things like, 'What would I really want to do if Jimmy Savile "fixed it" for me?' In response I keep coming up with the fantasy of conducting either a world famous symphony orchestra – or the world famous Black Dyke Mills Brass Band. No doubt that must say something about my personal need to control things. But, more truthfully, it reflects my image of prayer and how it fits into the scheme of things. When I pray I am not on my own, desperately trying to put a plug in with God either for myself or for some other more worthy cause. Rather I am responding to his prompting. I am making my distinctive contribution – even though it might appear to have all the significance of a single tap on a triangle – which is caught up in the full, beautiful, exhilarating and harmonious offering that is being made towards God.

I think the writer of one of our best loved hymns expressed it superbly well:

> As o'er each continent and island
> The dawn leads on another day,
> The voice of prayer is never silent
> Nor dies the strain of praise away.

Prayer is for many 'the way in' to God. To enter that way: to go through that door brings us into touch with one who is not only our Creator and worthy of our worship; he is also our Father and welcomes us in friendship and love.

## Questions

1. Why is it that people who claim no allegiance or specific relationship to God nevertheless feel it right to pray to him?
2. Since God loves us and knows our needs is it necessary to pray to him for anything?
3. Does God always answer our prayers? Is he bound to answer them?
4. What do you think prayer does – for us and for God?
5. How do you think God copes when individuals or different Christian groups pray for diametrically opposed answers?

## 2

# What Kind of God?
*Our view of God – image and reality*

Hands together. Eyes closed. Heads bowed. Most, if not all, of my readers will readily recall this formula as the prelude to prayers at school assembly. As we reached our early teens it was also the cue for the big 'switch off' and marked an ideal opportunity for glancing furtively at some forbidden literature or for pulling faces at our neighbour. But in our primary school-days we were much more compliant. This cryptic set of instructions in preparation for 'talking to God' was obeyed to the letter, though we rarely if ever contemplated the outcome or monitored the result. God was alive and well and good if the sun shone for the school sports. If it rained we conveniently forgot that we had asked for a fine day!

The conducting of school assemblies today, especially in a multi-faith school, is a very considerable work of art and I am full of admiration for the sensitive skill of teachers in producing the beautiful and meaningful acts of worship I have witnessed. It is a task considered too difficult to entrust to a bishop and so I am usually relegated to the substitutes' bench and 'wheeled on' only to do the final blessing.

## A PROFOUND QUESTION . . .

But it is at that point, when I am standing in front of a veritable rainbow of young and eager faces, which may include adherents of five different religions, that I am faced with a profound question. What kind of God are we worshipping? What images of God are around in those lovely little heads in front of me? And how do they compare with the images that are around in this little head of mine?

Sometimes the children draw me pictures to help me understand the nature of their God. He (yes, on the whole it is still 'he') bears a remarkable resemblance to the God of my own primary school-days. He comes in all shapes and sizes but most frequently in the guise of a benign head teacher or in the form of a science-fictional character from outer space. On occasions he has even been dressed like a bishop! Indeed, following a recent visit of mine to a primary school, some parents were reliably informed by their children that God had been to see them. And one six-year-old boy left me in no doubt about the practical power of his God as I sat having a school meal with him, 'Bishop, if you eat up your rice pudding, you'll get hairs on your chest.' Lord, I believe, help thou my unbelief!

But there is an important issue here. Children, it seems, tend to worship a God created according to their own image. That is, in an image relevant to their particular world. *And so do many adults.*

For some, God is perceived as a managing director . . . 'I didn't get where I am today by being soft-hearted!' He works to a divine plan and there is little or no consultation – ours is not to reason why. He is the one who must be obeyed. Those who don't toe the line are likely to have their progress blocked, or be passed over when the perks are being distributed or patronage is being exercised. Like

15

a celestial Brown Owl, to change the simile, Brownie points are dispensed to those who behave and do as they are told. When sufficient points have been collected they may be exchanged for a seat on the Board – the ultimate promotion! It needs to be said, of course, that such a view is as far off the mark in regard to most managing directors as it is with reference to God.

The perception of some others is of a God with all the propensities of a *good luck charm*. If there is a crisis in prospect, a major decision to be made or some significant success to be gained, the smile or favour of God is considered desirable if not essential. A good deed or a sizeable donation might just swing it your way. I am sure I must be imagining things but when I am sitting on a bus or a train wearing my purple shirt and my clerical collar people avoid me like the plague. Only as a last resort will they sit beside me. But I don't seem to have the same problem when I am travelling by aeroplane. Apparently in those circumstances some consider it advantageous to be on speaking terms with someone who has influence with the Almighty!

Yet for others God appears to have the characteristics of a *heavenly superman*. In answer to their request he apparently 'zaps' in to find them a parking space when necessary, or even to deliver them from an inconvenient head cold, while appearing to be impervious to some of the more chronic ills which currently afflict humanity. Perhaps some words of that ebullient Methodist Colin Morris are pertinent at this point, 'We place intolerable limits upon God's freedom when we assume that he must always jump at our commands and appear on stage the moment we choose to raise the curtain.'

## LIMITED BY EXPERIENCE . . .

So the creating of God according to our own image of him is not something restricted to children. Adults are prone to the same temptation. Their images, perhaps, are slightly more sophisticated but in many cases they are not all that different from the images created by their children. And they all suffer from the same inherent weakness, namely, they are determined by the limits of our experience.

A woman came to me recently and, in the forthright manner typical of my Yorkshire environment, expressed her disappointment at my size and my age. She said, 'I listen to you regularly on the *Derek Jameson Breakfast Show*, and, by the sound of your voice, I imagined that you were much taller and much younger.' Some people have a real gift of encouragement! Such colourful and constructive comments do wonders for one's self-esteem. But it just goes to illustrate that images created on the basis of limited experience are almost always bound to fall short of reality. To some extent this is true even when we look to the Scriptures to try to discover what God is like. For although in the world of the Bible we move from our immature fantasies about God towards reality as God has revealed it, the particular experience of the person or community concerned had a considerable bearing on their image of God.

I am sure that some of my readers will have been unfortunate enough to be on the receiving end of sermons or talks about the nature of God when words like 'infinite', 'omniscient' and 'omnipresent' have been flying consistently overhead. I find myself instinctively 'ducking' every time I hear them! But the interesting thing about such words is that they don't appear in the Bible. On the contrary, God is identified and his nature defined in terms of his relationship to individuals or communities and his action on their behalf.

God is not some absentee landlord who never appears. Nor is he some abstract force which cannot be described. He involves himself in human affairs. He reveals himself as one who has personal dealings with individuals and who enters into relationship with them. As the human story unfolds in the book of Genesis he quickly becomes known, for instance, as the God of Abraham, the God of Isaac and the God of Jacob. That is, the God who reveals himself in his dealings with, and in his activities on behalf of, these central figures in the history of the human race.

God didn't fire propositional pellets down from heaven, as it were, containing statements about himself for people to read. On the contrary he wrapped up his truths, including those about his own nature, in people and in his dealings with individuals, communities and nations. The image of God which people developed, therefore, was inevitably locked into their experience of him. So, for instance, when God speaks to Abram in Genesis (15:1) he says, 'Do not be afraid, Abram! I am your shield . . .'. In other words he was not some unknown God, but rather the same God who had revealed himself as Abram's shield and protector during a recent battle.

## HE DOESN'T LET GO . . .

That principle of God being identified within specific historical contexts is repeated again and again throughout the Bible. For instance, it is generally accepted that some of the early chapters of the book of Genesis were written at a time when the children of Israel were in captivity. Exiled in a foreign land they were in danger of being overwhelmed by a mood of despair and hopelessness.

In order to counteract such depression they reminded themselves of *God as Creator* – 'In the beginning God made heaven and earth'. In those early chapters the writers went on to emphasise the Creator's power in bringing order out of chaos; his care in paying great attention to detail; and his faithfulness in refusing to abandon his creation. It is a theme picked up by another writer during the isolation and apparent forsakenness of captivity:

> But Zion said, 'The Lord has forsaken me,
>     my Lord has forgotten me.'
> 'Can a woman forget her suckling child,
>     that she should have no compassion
>         on the son of her womb?'
> Even these may forget,
>     yet I will not forget you.
>
>                     Isaiah 49:14,15 (RSV)

One of the first wedding services I ever conducted happened to be that of a West Indian couple. Delores and Winston were great characters and I felt privileged to be allowed a share in their nuptials. The one feature of that service which I can remember to this day was Delores' response to my question, 'Wilt thou have this man to thy wedded husband . . . ?' She simply couldn't wait for me to complete the question before interrupting me and, with that lovely Caribbean intonation, enthusiastically and rather seductively saying, 'I will'. Here, I thought, was the beginning of a happy and lifelong marriage. I couldn't have been further from the truth for within three weeks Delores was media headlines. In a fit of temper she had hit Winston over the head with her shoe – a miracle in itself since he was six foot four and she was only four foot eleven! She was bound over to keep the peace but couldn't quite manage it and so the marriage was ended and they went their separate ways.

God is not like that. According to the Scriptures he is not changeable but faithful. He keeps faith with people. Indeed, he is called a *covenant* God. That is one who enters into agreement with people and keeps his promises. Even though people fail to keep faith with him he refuses to renege on his promise to them. No matter what it costs, he remains true. It is worth noting that it was that aspect of God's character which inspired the infant Church to share their faith in all the world. 'All authority in heaven and on earth has been given to me. Go, therefore, make disciples of all nations . . . And look, *I am with you always; yes, to the end of time*' (Matthew 28:18–20).

## IMAGES GALORE . . .

There is no shortage of images in the Scriptures. All of them give an insight into some aspect of the nature and character of God. And all of them spring out of the personal experience of those to whom God has revealed himself in his dealings with them.

### . . . God is Shepherd

He became known as 'the Shepherd of Israel', e.g. 'Shepherd of Israel, listen, you who lead Joseph like a flock' (Psalm 80:1).

Forty of the most formative years in the history of the emerging people of God were spent wandering in the wilderness following their escape from slavery in Egypt. Guidance and sustenance were the twin priorities of that people. Right from the beginning God was the Shepherd who accompanied them, providing them with light and food for the journey.

Psalm 23, the best known of all the psalms, has the shepherd as its central image. 'The Lord is my shepherd' is really a sublime poem about God. Of course, it is only one man's experience of God but its universal popularity testifies to the reality of God in other people's experience. The shepherd image was born out of a deep personal and community experience of a God who through all the vicissitudes of life reveals himself as *a God who cares*.

The extent to which he cares was given personal and visible expression in the life and ministry of Jesus Christ. We shall be looking in greater detail at the person of Jesus in our next chapter but it is sufficient at this point to note that he, who revealed the character of God in a quite unique way, declared himself to be *the Good Shepherd*, the depth of whose care was measured by his willingness to give his life for the sheep.

## . . . God is King

Alongside the pastoral image of God as *Shepherd* must be placed a more majestic image – that of God as *King*. It was Lord Blanch, a former Archbishop of York who said, 'The theme of the Bible can be summed up in four monosyllabic words: "The Lord is King." ' There are times when that conviction appears to be little more than an expression of nationalistic feeling i.e. God is for 'us' rather than 'them'. Generally, however, it went much deeper than that and God is acknowledged and worshipped as the Sovereign Lord; King not only of the people of Israel, but King of all the earth – and of the universe as well. This is nowhere more clearly expressed than in Psalm 47:

For Yahweh, the Most High, is glorious,
the great king over all the earth . . .
For he is king of the whole world . . .
God reigns over the nations . . .

vv. 2, 7, 8

But these specific words of the psalmist simply underline a truth that is clearly taught throughout the whole Bible – from his Kingship over creation at the beginning of time to the exercise of his sovereign judgement at the end of time.

Such a strong conviction is really quite astonishing in the light of the context in which it developed. The world of the Bible was different from ours but there were many similarities – including conflict between nations, economic disorder, injustice, selfishness and greed, to say nothing of the universal problems of sickness, senility and death. In the midst of such things to hold with conviction and tenacity to the belief that God was King of all the earth, and that he controlled it with love and mercy, was truly amazing. Yet, hold to it they did and it shaped their history and their destiny. Perhaps even more amazing was the revelation of the contrast between God's Kingship and that portrayed by earthly monarchs. He was a Servant-King, not so much concerned with the exercise of his own power as with serving the needs of ordinary people.

There is a host of other images which the Bible uses to reveal the character of God. He is *a Potter* who, through circumstance and experience, patiently fashions the lives of his creatures. He is *a Judge* whose concern is for justice, peace and right dealing between individuals and nations. He is *a Rock* on whom we can rely to find shelter and security in the midst of life's storms.

*. . . God is Father*

But one of the most common and helpful images of God
is that of *Father*. God's relationship to his people is as close
as that of a father to his child – though, it needs to be
said, the relationship is also compared to that between an
infant and its mother (Psalm 131:2). One of the best known
references to the Fatherhood of God in the Old Testament
is found in Psalm 103 – and even there it is not without
its 'motherly' traits!

> As a father has compassion on his children
> > so the Lord has compassion on those who fear
> > > him;
> for he knows how we are formed,
> > he remembers that we are dust.
>
> > > > > > v. 13 (NIV)

And it is not without significance that when Jesus was
asked by his disciples to teach them to pray he encouraged
them to begin with the term so familiar to him – *'Our
Father'*.

But the finest and most graphic portrayal of God as
Father is thought by many to be that given by Jesus in his
parable about the Prodigal Son in Luke 15.

It is a marvellous story told by the world's greatest
story-teller and it opens a wonderful window onto the
nature of God as Father.

*It's the way he tells them . . .*

The prodigal son goes off with all his money and blows
the lot on having a good time until, finally, he doesn't
have two pennies to rub together and he has to go to
work or starve to death. He gets a job on a pig farm and

keeps at it long enough to notice that the pigs are getting a better deal than he is, so he decides to go home.

There's nothing that's either clever or good about his decision. There's no sign that he realised he's made an ass of himself. No awareness that he's nearly broken his father's heart. No indication that he's sorry for what he has done. Nothing to suggest that he's decided to make amends and do better next time. He decides to go home for the simple reason that he will get three square meals a day – and for a man who's close to starvation, that's reason enough.

So he sets out on the return trip and on the way rehearses the speech he hopes will soften the old man's heart enough – so that at least he won't slam the door in his face. 'Father, I have sinned against heaven and before you. I am no longer worthy to be called your son.' That will soften the old man, if anything will, and he goes over it, rehearsing it in his mind. And just about the time he's got it off perfect, his father sees him coming and runs towards him. Before the boy has time to get so much as the first words out, the old man throws his arms around him and all but knocks him off his feet – with his tears and the incredulous laughter of his welcome.

The boy is back. That's all that matters. Who cares why he's back? The old man doesn't do what other fathers would be inclined to do. He doesn't say, 'I hope you've learned your lesson', nor 'I told you so'. He doesn't say, 'I hope you're finally ready to settle down'. Nor does he try the old tear-jerker, 'I hope there's some way you're going to make it up to your mother!' He just says, 'Quick, bring him something to eat. Fetch him some clothes to put on.' And when the boy finally manages to slip his prepared remarks into the conversation, the old man doesn't even hear them – he's in such a state. All he can say is that the boy was dead and is alive, was lost and is found. Then at the end of the scene, as Jesus tells it, they begin to make merry. They turn on the stereo, roll back the carpet, ring up the neighbours and have a party!

There's more . . . but I hope I have told you enough to whet your appetite to read the story for yourself. You will discover that the story is really all about the wonderful generosity of God our Father who refuses to stop loving us and always keeps his arms of acceptance and welcome open to us.


## GOD HAS THE LAST WORD – AND THE LAST LAUGH . . .

The profusion of images and models of what God is like is an indication of the inadequacy of our language to describe and the inability of our minds to grasp what God is really like. Though in the person of Jesus Christ, as we shall see in the next chapter, God revealed himself to us in a very special way our knowledge of him is still incomplete. It cannot be otherwise. He is always larger than our image of him. Always greater than our experience of him. The further I go on my Christian pilgrimage the more I become aware of how little I know and how much there is still to learn of God. I am constantly surprised and delighted by fresh insights into his nature and character. In this connection some words from Fynn's *Mister God, This is Anna* are particularly apt:

When you're little you 'understand' Mister God . . . Later on you understand him to be a bit different . . . Even though you understand him, he doesn't seem to understand you! . . . In whatever way or state you understand Mister God, so you diminish his size . . .

So Mister God keeps on shedding bits all the way

through your life until the time comes when you admit freely and honestly that you don't understand Mister God at all. At this point you have let Mister God be his proper size and wham, there he is laughing at you.

Though I believe God is personal, he is not a human being nor can he be fully understood in human terms. If that is so we had better let him have the last word:

> To whom can you compare me,
> or who is my equal? says the Holy One.
>
> Did you not know? Had you not heard?
> Yahweh is the everlasting God,
> he created the remotest parts of the earth.
> He does not grow tired or weary,
> his understanding is beyond fathoming.

Isaiah 40:25, 28, 29

## Questions

1. Does it matter if our image of God is not quite accurate?
2. Christians are very adamant that we all need God. Do you think that he needs us?
3. The story of the Prodigal Son revealed the generosity of God towards the one who strayed from home but do you think that he was just a little unfair to the one who didn't?
4. Do you think that God is really concerned about the trivial things of life or is it only significant matters that interest him?
5. Knowing us better than we know ourselves, could God keep going without a sense of humour?

# 3

# Love Came Down at Christmas
*The Word became flesh, he lived among us*

*His birth divides history.* His life forms the theme of epic films, record-breaking musicals and a host of best-selling novels. His name is used to swear and to bless, to revile as well as revere. Yet, to the majority of people he remains an enigma – an example to point to but not to follow; a setter of standards that are laudable but impractical; a significant figure of history but with little contemporary relevance. But he won't go away! My Christian, Jewish, Hindu, Sikh, Muslim and pagan friends all send me cards to mark his birth – an historical happening which is celebrated and observed the world over. A remarkable achievement for a child born to a peasant woman in the relative obscurity of an animal shelter attached to a wayside inn in Palestine nearly two thousand years ago.

I refer, of course, to Jesus Christ. Of whom, it seems, most of the world lives in blissful ignorance for eleven months of the year before going wild with excitement and expectancy in the month of December. During that particular month the interest in the baby Jesus is intense. It's almost as though there was a universal conspiracy to hide the fact that the baby ever grew to be a man. The story of the babe in the manger is what captivates the imagination. As we shall see, that humble birth forms a crucial part of the greatest story ever told, which inspires devotion and worship in the hearts of Christians the world over. But in society at large the story is sentimentalised, fantasised and commercialised almost beyond recognition. In the Western world particularly the celebration of the birth of Jesus is increasingly accompanied by a kind of financial and indulgent madness. A determination on the part of millions to spend more, eat more and drink more than is good for them and leading them to make such amazingly reassuring comments as, 'I'm glad Christmas only comes once a year' and 'I'll be relieved when it's all over'!

And it soon is of course. With the first of January (apart from a few notable exceptions, e.g. Scotland) comes the big 'switch off'. Not only of the Christmas lights but also of the Christmas spirit. The Christmas decorations are stored away until next year. And so too, it seems, is the baby Jesus.

## NOT RESTRICTED TO DECEMBER . . .

But, as the opening sentences of this chapter indicated, there is more to Jesus than can be encapsulated in two weeks in December. No ordinary baby could attract such world-wide devotion on the part of millions throughout the ages. No ordinary baby could become the object of such universal interest and activity. There is good reason, of course, why so much attention is focused on the birth of Jesus. A life which by any standards was remarkable, as we shall see, demands some explanation with regard to its beginnings. Any child left on a doorstep becomes the topic of emotive speculation. But when the baby Jesus was placed 'on the doorstep of the world' on that first Christmas morning it provided a wonder and a mystery that has fascinated humanity ever since.

Regarding his coming into the world a great variety of

explanations have been offered, ranging from the ridiculous to the sublime. I have heard children describe the arrival of Jesus into this world in terms of an E.T.-like appearance from outer space, while many adults are unshakeable in their sincerely held conviction that Jesus is nothing more and nothing less than the natural son of Mary and Joseph. Indeed they see such a truth as essential to the true manhood of Jesus. Otherwise, they insist, he was just a 'pretend' man and not the real thing. A kind of godly undercover agent who adopted a human disguise. Others hold firmly to the belief that Jesus began life as an ordinary baby but became extraordinary when he was 'taken over' by God to do his special work in the world.

## . . . *Traditional belief*

So many aspects of the birth of Jesus are surrounded in mystery – how could it be otherwise? Even the Gospel records of Matthew and Luke treat it in different ways. Nevertheless I believe that the weight of what evidence there is points to a unique beginning to his life on earth. Traditionally it is referred to as the 'Virgin Birth' but is more accurately described as 'the virginal conception' i.e. Jesus was conceived in the womb of the Virgin Mary without the intervention of a human father. Here is how Matthew describes the event:

> This is how Jesus Christ came to be born. His mother Mary was betrothed to Joseph; but before they came to live together she was found to be with child through the Holy Spirit. Her husband Joseph, being an upright man and wanting to spare her disgrace, decided to divorce her informally. He had made up his mind to do this when suddenly the angel of the Lord appeared to him in a dream and said, 'Joseph son of David, do not

29

be afraid to take Mary home as your wife, because she has conceived what is in her by the Holy Spirit. She will give birth to a son and you must name him Jesus, because he is the one who is to save his people from their sins.' Now all this took place to fulfil what the Lord had spoken through the prophet:

> Look! the virgin is with child
> and will give birth to a son
> whom they will call Immanuel,

a name which means 'God-is-with-us'. When Joseph woke up he did what the angel of the Lord had told him to do: he took his wife to his home; he had not had intercourse with her when she gave birth to a son; and he named him Jesus.

1:18–25

These words clearly teach that Jesus was uniquely conceived. Is that the secret of his remarkable life? We shall see.


THE PROPER MAN . . .

As I began to write this chapter a five-year-old acquaintance of mine gave me a little assistance. He came rushing home from Sunday School to engage in a slightly garbled and excited conversation with his dad. As you know parents can't resist the temptation to ask their children, 'Now, what did you learn today?' The five-year-old had no hesitation in extolling the virtues of God as he had understood them in Sunday School, 'God's a wonderful man, daddy. He made the birds, the flowers, the trees and all the animals. And daddy,' he said excitedly, 'he made you and me.' 'Really', said dad. 'Yes,' he replied, 'and mummy too.'

At that particular point his little face puckered and he continued with that boldness and lack of inhibition for which five-year-olds are famous, 'Mind you, I think he's a bit lazy at times for he lets Jesus do all the work for him.' 'Oh,' said his dad, trying to maintain some semblance of solemnity, 'and what's Jesus like?' 'Oh, he's super,' said the five-year-old, 'a magician, just like Paul Daniels – only better.'

In that simple and true story are many of the ingredients that have made up the debate about Jesus through the centuries. What was the nature of the relationship between God and Jesus? Was Jesus a miracle-worker or a mere man? Was he so different from 'normal' people as to disqualify him from being a realistic example to follow? Besides, living so long ago, has he anything pertinent to say to me today – apart from being a better performer than Paul Daniels?

### . . . Truly man

The first point that needs to be emphasised is the reality of the human nature of Jesus. He was no heavenly bionic man who was unrestricted by the normal frailties of the flesh. On the contrary he grew weary while walking the paths of Palestine. He was so tired that he fell asleep in the back of the boat while his travelling companions were having a rough time in the middle of a storm. He grew hungry and needed food. He developed thirst and asked for water.

He experienced the changing moods to which all of us are prone. He was deeply moved by innocent suffering and frustrated by pettifogging regulations. He was angry when the poor were exploited and annoyed with the

31

prejudices of the religious. He became sad and tearful at the graveside of a friend and appeared to baulk at the prospect of his own death. He knew times of success and times of failure. Throughout his life on earth he lived with the paradox of great power on the one hand and great vulnerability on the other. As a child he lay helpless in his mother's arms and begged for milk. As a man he hung helpless on the cross and felt forsaken by God. As an itinerant teacher there were times when he didn't know where the next meal or the next bed was coming from. He was known as 'the strong Son of God' but he was also the very vulnerable and very human son of Mary. *Jesus was truly man*.

### . . . Truly credible

I am a frequent visitor to London and therefore a regular user of the London Underground. My abiding memory of that experience is the loudly insistent reminder from the train-driver or station guard to 'Mind the gap' – a warning to travellers lest they fail to notice the gap which exists between the stationary train and the platform. To fail to heed the warning can have unfortunate consequences. It is a parable of human life. All of us, including the best of us, are conscious of the credibility gap which exists between our words and our actions. And if we're not aware of it our friends are, though they may be too kind to tell us. Inconsistency and hypocrisy are common to us all.

But in Jesus no such credibility gap existed. Even his opponents and enemies could find no fault in him. There was a wholeness about him which was impressive. He suffered no personal hang-ups and his personality was integrated and balanced. This is how one writer described his adolescent years: 'Jesus increased in wisdom, in stature, and in favour with God and with people' (Luke 2:52). A wonderfully perceptive statement of the intellectual, physical, spiritual and social development of his early years which was confirmed in later life and particularly during the three short years of his public ministry.

Just as his conception and birth were out of the ordinary so also it seems were his life and character. He has been described as *the proper man* or, to use a technical term, *the paradigm man* i.e. the 'example, pattern or representative man'. The kind of person God created us to be. The Bible tells us clearly that humankind was created in the image of God. All of us, men and women, reveal some aspect of that likeness but only in Jesus do we see the true image of God *and* man. In Jesus alone we see the full possibilities of human existence when it is lived for and with God. Jesus is the kind of person God intends us to be. Far from having little practical relevance it seems that his balanced life and integrated personality can inspire us with hope regarding our own true destiny whether we are man or woman.

## LIVING UP TO HIS NAME . . .

If Jesus was an extraordinary man then his name gives us the clue to the extraordinary nature of the work he came to do. Today we use names rather like personal labels. In Bible days names had much greater significance. Frequently they expressed a longing on the part of parents for their child to be endowed with special character and capacity. In the case of human parents this could only be a pious hope. With God it was different. When he named, or renamed, people the hope expressed in their name was fulfilled. This was particularly so in the case of Jesus whose name was just another form of Joshua, a favourite name in Israel at the time which, in Hebrew, means 'he will save'.

So when the Virgin Mary is given the astounding news that she is to become the mother of the Son of God, to Joseph is given the responsibility of giving him the name by which he was to be called. A name which would not only declare his character and capacity but also express the true hope of the nation which he was to fulfil: 'She will give birth to a son and you must name him Jesus, because he is the one who is to save his people from their sins' (Matthew 1:21).

I can still recall the words of the little chorus I learned as a boy which, though simply expressed, helped me to grasp at an early age something of the nature of the special work that Jesus had come to do:

> He did not come to judge the world,
> He did not come to blame,
> He did not only come to seek,
> It was to save he came.
> And when we call him *Saviour*
> *we call him by his name.*

### . . . A strange paradox

There is a strange paradox here. This former carpenter of Nazareth; this man who extolled meekness, self-denial and humility; this travelling teacher who stooped to wash the dirt off others' feet and who refused to defend himself in the face of false accusation and cruel death, became extrovert and outspoken in fulfilling his calling as *Saviour*.

'I am the Light of the world', he said (John 8:12). In other words he claimed that he was *the Light* in which all else is illuminated and without which nothing ultimately makes sense. Some claim for a humble carpenter.

'I am the Bread of Life', he declared (John 6:35). Just as bread or its equivalent is the necessary 'staff of life' throughout the world, so Jesus declares himself to be necessary for the true life of humankind. Some claim for a man born in obscurity!

'Come to me, all you who labour and are overburdened, and I will give you rest. Shoulder my yoke and learn from me, for I am gentle and humble in heart, and you will find rest for your souls. Yes, my yoke is easy and my burden light' (Matthew 11:28–30). In other words he claims the ability to remove crushing burdens and offers his own gentle mastery in exchange. Some claim and some offer from a man who was self-effacing!

### . . . No credibility gap here

Jesus not only made remarkable claims – he also delivered the goods. Here again there was no credibility gap between his words and his deeds. Time and time again he lived up to his name to save and to deliver. He brought peace to the fearful, health to the sick and life to the dead. His power to save was not reserved for the souls of individuals nor his ability to deliver restricted to their physical needs. As Saviour his calling was to set people free from fear of every kind.

But faced with a multitude of human needs he didn't forget that his basic task was 'to save his people from sins'. He was as much concerned to set people free from envy and pride, anger and covetousness as he was to heal the sick and comfort the sorrowful. He was free from prejudice. He saw good in Zacchaeus, a man involved in financial trickery (Luke 19) and in the Woman of Samaria who had been divorced five times (John 4). But he insisted on putting his finger upon the selfishness of their lives in order to bring them healing and wholeness. He refused to treat the symptoms and ignore the disease. He was the transformer of human life. Whatever he touched he made whole. That is the essence of salvation. He was Saviour by name and Saviour by nature.

*. . . Get up . . . and go . . .*

On one occasion Jesus was approached by four men carrying their friend on a stretcher (Mark 2). The man was paralysed and unable to walk but they were determined to get him to Jesus, believing that he was the only one who could heal him. Because of the crowds surrounding Jesus they had difficulty getting to him but their persistence won the day and eventually they placed the stretcher carrying their friend in front of him – and waited to see what Jesus would do. I have no doubt that they and others in the crowd expected a word or touch from Jesus that would heal the man's paralysis. But they got a surprise when Jesus said, 'My child, your sins are forgiven.' And no one was more surprised than the man himself, indeed, I can imagine him thinking to himself, 'It's not my sins I'm bothered about, it's my legs. I can't walk!'

At this point some of the critics of Jesus began to complain that he was stepping out of line by claiming to forgive sins. As far as they were concerned, to forgive sins was the prerogative of God and Jesus was a usurper. Jesus didn't argue. He simply asked whether it was easier to claim something, like the forgiveness of sins, the reality of which could not visibly be tested, or something, like the cure of paralysis, which clearly could be tested. The implication is clear: if Jesus' word can cure the man of his paralysis, then who can deny that he can also forgive him? To prove the point, and to endorse the claim which he had made, Jesus said to the paralytic, ' "I order you: get up, pick up your stretcher, and go off home." And the man got up, and at once picked up his stretcher and walked out in front of everyone, so that they were all astonished and praised God saying, "We have never seen anything like this" ' (vv. 11–12).

Over the centuries since Jesus came great debates have been held and thousands, perhaps millions, of books have been written about the mechanics of forgiveness. How does Jesus actually forgive sins? Strangely enough the concern of the New Testament lies more with the fact of forgiveness than with the theory. The one thing which is clear above all else is that it is part of God's nature to forgive. Indeed he desires to forgive our sins. As the story above makes clear, Jesus is not only interested in healing the body, he is committed to bringing wholeness to our entire personality – and that includes the forgiveness of our sins. He not only has authority to forgive sins – he actually does it!

## LOVE CAME DOWN AT CHRISTMAS . . .

But his power 'to save his people from their sins' was not some impersonal force which dominated people and manipulated them to do his will so that they had no option but to obey. Such power was totally foreign to him. He had deliberately turned his back upon it at the very beginning of his public ministry when he resisted the devil's temptations in the wilderness (Matthew 4). The whole thrust of those temptations was to induce him to overwhelm people with irresistible force and to manipulate them with psychological pressure. The diabolical reasoning behind it went something like this, 'If you want to win friends and influence people then you must be prepared to use and even misuse power to achieve results. The ends justifies the means.' Jesus would have none of it. He who entered the stage of history as a baby in a cattle shed yet who was designated by God as the Saviour of the human race chose to lead people rather than drive them. And he led them by *the power of love*.

This was the abiding characteristic of his life, an amazing love which was extended to all, friend and foe alike. A love which was totally without self-interest. It gave, looking for nothing in return. It had no pre-conditions. It didn't coerce. It didn't smother people, place them under obligation or put them under psychological pressure. It was love which affirmed them as people but left them free to respond. A simple example of this unselfconscious love which had such power to save can be seen in John 5 where, at the Pool of Bethesda, Jesus delivers an afflicted man from the crippling power of paralysis. There is no self-advertising, crowd-attracting, public display on the part of Jesus. Just a loving and personal application of his power to heal. Then, in the midst of the crowd surrounding the pool, he stole quietly away. So unobtrusively, in fact, that the man didn't even know who had healed him.

*. . . Love so amazing*

But, of course, the supreme example of the love of Jesus is to be seen at the cross. Here we are at the very heart of the matter. Here, according to the Scriptures, we have the key to the salvation of the world and to Jesus' calling to be the Saviour. Deep mystery surrounds the events of that first Good Friday. Any suggestion that we could possibly plumb the depths of that mystery would leave us open to the charge of arrogance. Yet there is one thing that seems beyond question. Whatever was taking place at Calvary that day God was in control and love was supreme.

Oh, there was a lot of hate about also. There was lots

of anger and remorse, loads of frustration and guilt, a deep sense of failure and an incredible amount of self-righteousness. The cross was surrounded by all kinds of emotion but as one listens to and watches the central figure one is forced to the conclusion that despite the apparent 'foolishness' of the cross love is in control. It was love in action. Reaching out in forgiveness to those who were driving in the nails: 'Father, forgive them for they know not what they do.' Reaching out in mercy to the thief whose wrongdoing had condemned him to death: 'Today you will be with me in Paradise.' Reaching out in sympathy and understanding towards his mother and commending her to the 'bereavement after-care' of John the disciple: 'Woman, behold your son . . . son, behold your mother.' The very shape and symbol of the cross speaks volumes to us of the love of God which reaches down from heaven to earth and whose arms are stretched wide to embrace the whole world. As the passiontide hymn reminds us:

> See from his head, his hands, his feet,
> Sorrow and love flow mingling down:
> Did e'er such love and sorrow meet,
> Or thorns compose so rich a crown?

## . . . So divine

Perhaps it is at this point that we reach the heart of the mystery. There had been a developing awareness on the part of the disciples that this Jesus was someone a bit special. In the light of their experience of his words and deeds and companionship the question that persistently comes to their minds is, 'Who is this man?' Indeed on one occasion, when in the midst of the storm he saves them from disaster, they specifically articulate the question,

'Who can this be? Even the wind and the sea obey him' (Mark 4:35–41). They were beginning to get a glimmer of the answer to their own question – and I think they were awed and perhaps a little worried by it!

You see, the disciples of Jesus, like him, were devout Jews. They believed passionately that there was only one God; yet circumstances and experience were forcing them to the inevitable conclusion that 'this Jesus' was also divine. His words, his deeds, his unique relationship to God the Father to which he frequently laid claim and which some of them had witnessed, for example in the mysterious experience of the Transfiguration (see Mark 9:2–8), all pointed in the same direction. Eventually Peter became the spokesman for them all when, in answer to Jesus' question, 'Who do you say I am?', he replied, 'You are the Christ, the Son of the living God' (Matthew 16:16). That confession of Peter's has been taken up by the universal Church throughout the ages. Jesus Christ is the Son of God. Jesus is both man and God. He is both human and divine. Nothing less can account for the brief but basic creed which undergirded the life and witness of the early church – *Jesus Christ is Lord*.

Now we can perhaps begin to understand why his love was so amazing. It was *divine love*. Jesus embodied the love of God. It was God's own love that was displayed in Jesus. As Paul wrote in his letter to the Romans, 'It is proof of God's own love for us, that Christ died for us while we were still sinners' (Romans 5:8). No preconditions here. God loved us so much that he gave his only Son – not because we had earned such love or deserved such love, but because he is God and he really does love us.

Can you see the wonder of it? This man whose birth divides history dies at the crossroads of history as the Saviour of the world. He is man and he is God and he is love. He was never more human than at the cross. He was never more divine than at Calvary. Here, therefore, is the glorious and reassuring truth. We are not in the hands of a blind and cruel fate. There is love at the heart of the universe – and his name is *Jesus*.

## LOVE AROSE AT EASTER . . .

It was Paul in his sublime poem about love in 1 Corinthians 13 who said, 'Love never comes to an end.' As darkness began to fall on the evening of that first Good Friday the opposite seemed to be true. Love, it appeared, had come to a rather sticky end. The one who personified love was dismissed from the world with cruelty and contempt by those who were consumed with hate and fear. It looked as though evil had triumphed over good. Love was defeated. Jesus was 'crucified, died and was buried'. His body lay in the solitude of the tomb while his friends mourned his death and the end of all their hopes. Love had promised so much and, it seemed, delivered so little. Even love could not conquer death. What price a Saviour who cannot save?

But God is full of surprises. Three days later, on the first Easter Day, Jesus rose from the dead and love triumphed over death. Of course, no one saw him rise and therefore we must not be over-precise about the detail of the actual resurrection. Indeed the detail differs from one account to another. But one thing is clear. All of the Gospels agree historically that Jesus rose from the dead. His disciples had refused to believe the promises of Jesus that he would rise from the dead. But when the Risen Jesus encountered them after his resurrection it put the matter beyond question. They had seen him crucified. They had seen him buried. Now they saw him alive and well! Death had not conquered love. On the contrary love had destroyed death. It could not be imprisoned by death. The love of God embodied in Jesus had been nailed to a cross. Now that same love embodied in the Risen Jesus burst out of the tomb and through the barrier of death on Easter morning. Jesus is Lord – even over death!

> Paul is right, love never comes to an end.
> Jesus is alive, therefore love has triumphed.
> God is love, therefore love is eternal.

## Questions

1. How would you explain to a child that Jesus is *not* 'just like Paul Daniels only better'?
2. Just how realistic is it to believe that Jesus truly appreciates all the weaknesses and failures and even the successes of ordinary human beings?
3. Given that God is our all-powerful Creator, don't you think it was a bit remiss of him to allow the world to get into such a mess that he had to mount a very costly 'Rescue Operation' by sending his Son to die for us?
4. Can you explain why the cross – which after all was a Roman gallows – has become such a world-wide symbol of love?
5. Would it matter if it was only the Spirit of Jesus that survived the crucifixion and his physical body remained in the tomb?

# God in the Present Tense
*Experiencing the Holy Spirit today*

In all my years of trying to teach others about God it was when I came to the doctrine of the Holy Spirit that I encountered the most difficulty. Looks of incomprehension would spread over the faces of my hearers as I resorted to clichés of religious jargon that failed to convince me, let alone them. Perhaps it cannot be otherwise. We are dealing here with a mystery and, perhaps, the fear of straying into heresy prevents us from being adventurous in our attempts to describe or explain the person and work of the Holy Spirit. Nevertheless I think it is worth a try.

## CONFUSION . . .

A few weeks ago I was the guest speaker at a local luncheon club. The welcome was warm but the initial comment of one of the members annoyed me at first. 'You are not as spiritual as your predecessors.' That's what he said and that, I presumed, was what he meant. Apparently I wasn't quite up to scratch, being more secular and less spiritual than those who had gone before me. That was the clear implication of his remark. Fortunately, just as I was about to climb onto my high horse (which had all the semblance of a war horse!), he explained what he meant. He was a local businessman and while at first it seemed as though he was denigrating me in comparison to previous Bishops of Bradford he assured me that his words were a strong affirmation of my involvement in local community issues, like the promotion of healthy race relations.

It was his use of the word 'spiritual' that caused confusion in my mind. He saw it as an appropriate term for so-called 'religious' activity but not, apparently, for the hurly-burly activity of normal life. And certainly not for the somewhat murky and messy business of involvement in social and political issues within the community. In actual fact my friend's comment, while at first confusing, was extremely perceptive. In reality he was debunking the false division between the so-called sacred and secular aspects of life. As our subsequent conversation revealed he was insisting that the proper place for the Christian was not hidden away in a churchy environment but in the everyday world of business, industry and commerce.

A similar confusion exists in the minds of many with regard to the term Holy Spirit. To whom or to what does it refer? Does the term refer to a mysterious ghostly person or a godly influence? Is it a powerful yet impersonal force which we can harness to our own advantage? Perhaps the greatest confusion of all and the one of which my friend was guilty concerns the place of the Holy Spirit in the scheme of life. Is he, or it, confined to the Church or is he at large in the world? Is he the exclusive possession of the 'spiritually élite' or is he available to all?

### . . . No afterthought

God's story, or a very important part of it, is to be found in the Bible. From the beginning that story involved the Spirit of God. The Spirit was not an afterthought. Indeed although the Holy Spirit came with power at a particular point in the life of the early church he has always been around and figures prominently in the Old Testament. There are two Hebrew words which are translated as 'spirit' in the English versions of the Bible. One of them means 'breath' and the other 'wind'. Though the second of them (*ruach*) may be the more significant in helping us to come to a clearer understanding of the Holy Spirit, both words serve to convey the meaning of God's ceaseless energy creating and sustaining the living world, including humankind. Nowhere is this more graphically portrayed than in Psalm 104:29–30:

> Turn away your face and they panic;
> take back their breath and they die
> and revert to dust.
> Send out your breath and life begins;
> you renew the face of the earth.

The Spirit is not just God's outgoing activity and energy, it is the very life of God upon which all other life depends. The Spirit is not confined to one place but rather is at large in the world. That seems to be the general view of the Old Testament. It was certainly the conviction of the writer of Psalm 139 based on his daily experience:

> Where shall I go to escape your spirit?
> Where shall I flee from your presence?
> If I scale the heavens you are there,
> if I lie flat in Sheol, there you are.
>
> If I speed away on the wings of the dawn,
> if I dwell beyond the ocean,
> even there your hand will be guiding me,
> your right hand holding me fast.

vv. 7–10

45

God knows us inside out. There is no escape from his Spirit.

*. . . No stranger*

Some years ago I sat alone on a steeply-banked shingle beach in Norfolk with the sea relentlessly rushing in with a roar and just as quickly retreating with the distinctive rumbling of pebbles realigning themselves on the shore. The sea, the sky and the stones were all a matching colour – dull grey. The wind was fresh. The beach was deserted. Yet there was an 'encounter' with my Creator which I was neither seeking nor expecting. To be alone was what I most wanted at that precise moment. But alone I was not – and I knew it.

It is difficult to explain. It was not a magical experience nor a mere flight of fancy. It was too 'tangible' for that, too 'real' to be so easily dismissed. The only way I can describe it is that a mysterious sense of the presence of God and the wonder of his creation and his amazing love for me filled my whole being. It was breath-taking. Awe-inspiring. Time stood still. There was a clarity of vision and understanding that I had never known before – as though a divine penny had dropped! Several months later some words written by John Taylor, formerly Bishop of Winchester, helped me put the experience in context:

> My own attempt to understand the Holy Spirit has convinced me He is active in precisely those experiences that are very common – experiences of recognition, sudden insight, and influx of awareness when you wake up and become alive to something. It may be another person, or a scientific problem, and suddenly the penny drops. Every time a human being cries, 'Ah, I see it now!', that's what I mean by the Holy Spirit.

I would stress that my experience on the Norfolk beach had much more the character of an encounter with a person than with a subjective communing with nature. Above all I was conscious that I was in the presence of someone greater than myself and in whose presence I was finding some kind of perspective and identity. In that particular sense I imagine that the Holy Spirit is no stranger to many of my readers.

## MYSTERIOUS BUT NOT VAGUE . . .

'Can you fathom the mysteries of God? Can you probe the limits of the Almighty?' Those rhetorical questions were asked by one of Job's Comforters (Job 11:7 NIV) and the implied answer was, 'Of course not. God is beyond our understanding and out of the reach of our analysis.' So also is the Spirit of God. Yet as we move from the Old Testament into the New the vagueness to a large extent disappears and the Spirit comes into much sharper focus. Much of the mystery remains but the diffuse and somewhat ill-defined portrait of the Spirit, as seen in the Old Testament, is replaced by a much clearer understanding of his nature and work. As we shall see this dramatic change is intimately connected with the coming of Jesus into the world.

### . . . Personal

One of the great New Testament 'discoveries' is the personal nature of the Spirit. No longer is the Spirit to be seen simply in terms of the outgoing activity of God. It includes that, of course, but it is much more. When we encounter the Spirit in the New Testament we are met not by an 'it' but by a 'he' – though it is worth noting at this point that the word *ruach* in Hebrew is feminine! The actions of the Holy Spirit are personal actions. He guides (John 16:13), he restrains (Acts 16:6), he distributes gifts as he wills (1 Corinthians 12:11) and he can be grieved (Ephesians 4:30). Thus some of the commonly accepted constituents of personality, namely, mind, feeling and will are attributed to the Spirit. Jesus himself uses the personal pronoun 'he' when referring to the Spirit. The Spirit no longer must be seen as an impersonal force or simply as a godly influence. He possesses personality.

### . . . Sovereign

We are given a very interesting insight into the character of the Holy Spirit in the Acts of the Apostles chapter 8. A man called Simon Magus is envious of the power of the Spirit which he witnesses in the actions of the apostles of Jesus. He longs to possess such power and offers to buy it from the apostles: 'When Simon saw that the Spirit was given through the laying on of the apostles' hands, he offered them money with the words, "Give me the same power so that anyone I lay my hands on will receive the Holy Spirit." '

Apparently he saw the Holy Spirit as an impersonal force which he could harness to his own selfish advantage. The apostles and, indeed, the rest of the New Testament make it abundantly clear that though the Holy Spirit may be 'discovered' he cannot be controlled. He is the Holy Spirit of God. *He is sovereign.* He distributes his gifts as he wills and not according to merit or as a result of manipulation. Like the wind, which is so often used as a symbol of the Spirit, he is sovereign and free. Indeed the followers of Jesus, through their contemporary experience, were forced to the conclusion that the Holy Spirit was not only personal and sovereign but that he was also divine.

As a result they had to live with a paradox. As devout Jews they believed in one God. Yet they viewed the Father, the Son and the Holy Spirit as divine but distinct. In the centuries after Christ the Church wrestled with the paradox and affirmed its belief in the mystery of the Holy Trinity – three Persons in one God. The first Christians didn't debate the theory they simply acknowledged the mystery in words like these, 'The grace of the Lord Jesus Christ, the love of God and the fellowship of the Holy Spirit be with you all' (2 Corinthians 13:13).

## THE GIFT OF GOD THE FATHER . . .

One of the most disappointing experiences I have ever had was during my early years as a vicar. A man of some considerable intelligence came into the regular worshipping life of the local church and began to show all the signs of a healthy and balanced development as a Christian disciple. It was a great privilege to be allowed to help in his Christian nurture and a very humbling experience to have one's help so eagerly sought and, apparently, so gratefully received. Unexpectedly my friend and 'student' arrived one morning to inform me that since we last met he had come to 'possess' the Holy Spirit. As a consequence he felt that there was nothing more he could learn from me. Rather arrogantly he told me that he was dispensing with my services immediately. Indeed there was a fairly strong hint that, perhaps, now that he 'possessed' the Spirit he could teach me a thing or two.

I call this incident disappointing not because it was a considerable blow to my self-esteem – though I would be dishonest if I denied such negative feelings – but because of the mistaken arrogance and lack of humility which provoked it. Though, thankfully, it is possible for individuals to receive the Holy Spirit and for him to dwell in the life both of the individual and the Church, it is rather unhealthy and somewhat misleading for either to believe that the Holy Spirit is in their possession. Far from being my, or the Church's, possession the Holy Spirit is God the Father's gift to us through Jesus Christ. In the light of such a wonderful gift there is room for neither arrogance nor pride.

*. . . Bringing life*

Arrogance and pride are out of place but not joy and thanksgiving. For God in giving us his Spirit shares with us his life. Every week throughout the world Christians of every race repeat one of the Church's great creeds which expresses belief in the Holy Spirit as 'The Lord, the Giver of Life'. Indeed it was the coming of the Holy Spirit that marked the birthday of – the giving of life to – the Church. That day, which had been promised for centuries, was known as the Day of Pentecost (see Acts 2) and marked the initial outpouring of God's Holy Spirit upon his Church. The Spirit came with special signs of wind and fire to give power to the Church for its witness to Jesus throughout the world. On that wonderful day the followers of Jesus were changed from being rather timid and fearful disciples into robust and outgoing messengers of God's Good News. The dramatic elements of that special coming of the Spirit will not necessarily accompany our experience of the Spirit today. Nevertheless the effects of that initial coming are repeated in every age. He brings life and renewal to disciples today just as he did on the Day of Pentecost.

I said a little earlier that with the coming of Jesus the Spirit of God was brought into sharper focus. Certainly there is an intimate connection between the Holy Spirit and the life and work of Jesus. Indeed, on occasions he is called the Spirit of Jesus. It was the Holy Spirit, the Lord and Giver of life, who activated and filled the life of Jesus. *His coming* into the world is linked with the Spirit, for the angel said to Mary, 'The Holy Spirit will come upon you, and the power of the Most High will cover you with its shadow. And so the child will be holy and will be called Son of God' (Luke 1:35). *His baptism* in the Jordan is linked with the Spirit, for 'As he was coming up out of the water, he saw the heavens torn apart and the Spirit, like a dove, descending on him' (Mark 1:9–10). *His public ministry* is inaugurated in the power of the Spirit for he begins his first sermon in his home synagogue with these words:

> The spirit of the Lord is on me,
> for he has anointed me
> to bring the good news to the afflicted.
> He has sent me to proclaim liberty to captives,
> sight to the blind,
> to let the oppressed go free,
> to proclaim a year of favour from the Lord.
>
> Luke 4:18–19

*His resurrection* (and ours) is linked with the Spirit for, as Paul writes in his letter to the Romans (8:11), 'If the Spirit of him who raised Jesus from the dead has made his home in you, then he who raised Christ Jesus from the dead will give life to your own mortal bodies, through his Spirit living in you.'

The Spirit who activated the life of Jesus and brought renewed life to his disciples is the same Holy Spirit who brings life to people today. He is the Giver of life and such a quality of life as can only come from God the Creator of all life.

*. . . Creating fellowship*

As I write this chapter a vivid memory comes rushing into mind. It concerns my early days as a young assistant curate in the parish of Crowborough in Sussex where, on one occasion, I was almost overwhelmed by the sense of unity and fellowship created by the Holy Spirit. The vicar and I were giving Holy Communion to those kneeling at the communion rail. As I gazed at the row of outstretched empty hands before me, I saw the hands of a garage attendant, a doctor, a solicitor, a carpenter, a diplomat, a teacher, a housewife, an engineer, a stockbroker, a milkman, a driving instructor and a lollipop lady. An amazing assortment of people but all with the common bond – the Holy Spirit. They shared in the life of God through his Holy Spirit.

The Holy Spirit not only gives life, he creates fellowship between people. He is the cord which binds the Church in one. Just as the various parts of the human body are linked by one bloodstream, so the members of the Church (for which another name is the Body of Christ) are linked and sustained by the one Holy Spirit. 'We were baptised into one body in a single Spirit' (1 Corinthians 12:13). Christians don't always share the same view about things but they do share in the same Holy Spirit. The Spirit which brings them life also knits them together into one family – the family of God.

THE INDISPENSABLE COMPANION . . .

Mary Peters, winner of the pentathlon in the Olympic Games, tells a lovely story about her coach, the late 'Buster' McShane. It is a particularly poignant story for me because 'Buster' and I were at school together and for the whole of our boyhood years lived in the same Belfast street. Mary tells how the high jump was of crucial importance to her in her attempt to win a medal. In the other four events her coach had been able to get close enough to her at the start in order to encourage and reassure her. For some reason this was not possible during the high jump and Mary felt disconsolate, alone and very much in need of Buster's companionship and inspiration. Together they solved the problem. He would stand as close as possible to the high jump arena and wear a brightly coloured jumper. It was a bright and somewhat dazzling yellow which stood out boldly and unmistakably in the crowd. As Mary prepared for her final crucial jump she glanced at the crowd, easily spotting the yellow jumper. She gained confidence from the sight of her coach who she knew would be eagerly rooting for her success. Inspired by his presence she jumped superbly well and went on to win the Olympic Gold Medal.

### . . . Something better than a yellow jumper

When Jesus was leaving his disciples to return to his Father in heaven, they were very disconsolate at the thought of being left alone to face a world hostile to their belief and way of life. Jesus promised them help. He said: 'I shall ask the Father, and he will give you another Paraclete to be with you for ever, the Spirit of truth . . .' (John 14:16). There is a wealth of meaning in that word 'paraclete' which, of course, refers to the Holy Spirit. In various parts of John's Gospel it is translated as helper, comforter, counsellor, intercessor, advocate. The translations are simply variations on a central theme. The core meaning of the word is 'one who comes alongside to help' as a friend and companion. More particularly it carries with it the imagery of one who stands by our side in a court of law and pleads our cause.

It would be a great mistake, as very many have discovered over the centuries since, to dismiss this promise of Jesus as of little consequence. Equipped with this promise, and the fulfilment of it which they experienced on the Day of Pentecost, these humanly inadequate disciples 'stood up and were counted' in the face of a hostile world. They won no gold medals for their trouble. On the contrary some of them were martyred and all of them were despised for the stand they took for truth, right living and justice. They had all the personality weaknesses that are common to men and women today. They were not plaster saints divorced from real life. Socially and intellectually the odds were stacked against them. In the eyes of the world they were born losers. Yet the fact that there is a universal Church of God in existence today is a remarkable witness to their courage, commitment and 'success'. It is an even greater testimony to the presence of the Paraclete, the power of the Holy Spirit, alongside them. He was their teacher, their guide, their helper, their indispensable companion who stood alongside them and strengthened and enabled them to spread the message of God's love throughout the world.

Millions of people throughout the centuries since and millions of people in our day and age can bear witness to the power of that same Holy Spirit as their indispensable companion. Not only the well-known modern saints, like Mother Teresa, Cicely Saunders, Terry Waite and a host of others, but a multitude of ordinary men and women, who live ordinary lives in an extraordinary manner with the help of the Holy Spirit.

NOT A SUBSTITUTE . . .

At this point it may be helpful to correct a mistaken view that some people have about the Holy Spirit. They see him as a replacement or substitute for Jesus. They feel that since Jesus had to return to his Father, the Holy Spirit was sent to make up for his absence. But that is far from the truth and, taken to its logical conclusion, turns the Holy Spirit into a kind of 'second best'. But the Holy Spirit was not given to make up for the absence of Jesus. On the contrary, he was given to intensify the presence of Jesus in the lives of his followers. Certainly that is how it worked out in practice. The disciples who at first were devastated at the prospect of their Lord's departure proceeded, with the help of the Holy Spirit, to 'turn the world upside-down'. They were convinced that Jesus was now more real to them than ever before. While Jesus was on earth he could only be in one place at one time. Yet with his going to the Father and the Holy Spirit's coming they felt the presence of Jesus continually with them.

*. . . But a spotlight*

There is one scene which never fails to bring out the goose-pimples on me and fill me with deep emotion. It is the sight and the sound of the lone piper on the ramparts of Edinburgh Castle during the Festival Tattoo. All around is intense darkness when suddenly the spotlight picks out, and throws into brilliant yet stark relief, the lone piper. Dr James Packer in his book *Keep in Step with the Spirit* uses the term 'floodlighting' to describe the work of the Holy Spirit. It carries the same imagery as the spotlight on my lone piper. The main concern of the Holy Spirit is not to make a name for himself but to pick out, portray and promote the characteristics of the life of Jesus. That's why the followers of Jesus in every age have known the presence of Jesus so obviously with them. It was this principal aspect of the Spirit's work to which Jesus referred before his death: 'However, when the Spirit of truth comes he will lead you to the complete truth, since he will not be speaking of his own accord . . . He will glorify me, since all he reveals to you will be taken from what is mine' (John 16:13, 14). It is this special ministry of 'spotlighting' Jesus that enables an historical figure to become a contemporary friend. It is not wishful thinking nor a grand delusion. Through the ministry of the Holy Spirit Jesus becomes real – today.

Indeed the Holy Spirit not only portrays the characteristics of Jesus he helps to produce them in the lives of ordinary people.

### . . . God in the present tense

Thus we return to the title of this chapter and to the truth it tries to convey. God the Father and Jesus Christ his Son are not imprisoned in the past. Through the ministry of the Holy Spirit they become part of our contemporary experience. 'Immanuel' was one of the prophetic names given to Jesus at the time of his birth (Matthew 1:23). The name means 'God-is-with-us'. It is the Holy Spirit who makes that ancient prophecy as much a reality in the twentieth century as he did in the first century.

Indeed the Holy Spirit brings both the past and the future into the present. For instance, Jesus promised his followers that he would never leave them nor forsake them but would be with them to the ends of the world and the end of the age. The Holy Spirit makes that promise come true. He comes alongside us and makes Jesus real and present to us today. He also does the same regarding God's promise concerning the future. Indeed he is, as it were, the first instalment, the guarantee that what has been promised will be fully realised. For instance, God the Creator purposed and Jesus the Saviour promised us life in all its fullness, 'I have come so that they might have life and have it to the full'. (John 10:10). The life to which Jesus refers is eternal life, the life of God, the life of the age to come. It is the Holy Spirit who brings that life into the here and now and enables us to share in it.

Thus we can say with appropriate humility and with genuine conviction: *God is here. His Spirit is with us.*

## Questions

1. Looking back over your life can you discern influences or happenings in the past that may be attributed to the presence of the Holy Spirit?
2. Do you think it matters if we can't fully explain or even understand the Holy Spirit?
3. Why do you think many people find it difficult to view the Holy Spirit in personal terms?
4. Suppose you are being interviewed for a new job or you are going to begin a new venture – just what kind of help would you ask or expect from the Holy Spirit?
5. Since the Holy Spirit is the Creator of fellowship how do you explain why so many Christians – even within the same church – fall out with each other?

# 5

## Sharing the Journey
### *The Church – a pilgrim people*

I am fortunate to be a member of a very large family. Indeed I am the youngest of fourteen children. You can imagine that with those numbers whoever was up first each morning in our working-class household was likely to be the best dressed for the day. I have vague recollections of a small house with a crowded dining table. Distant memories of multitudes of people, some of whom I later came to recognise as my brothers and sisters, coming in and out of the family home. I can recall times of laughter and tears, of noise and singing and the virtual impossibility of finding space and time to be alone. But it wasn't until my teen-age years and later that I began to realise just how privileged I was to be surrounded by such a large and happy family. And particularly now that so many of that family have died I am appreciating even more just how fortunate I was.

### A WORLD-WIDE FAMILY . . .

The amazing world-wide nature of the Family of God, which is another name for what you or I would call the Church, dawned on me in a similar way. During my time as a minister in parishes and then as an archdeacon I was always trying to help others to have a wider vision of the

Church. But it wasn't until I became a bishop that I began to grasp in a new way something of the universality of the Family of God.

It came to me with all the force of a hammer-blow when I attended my first Lambeth Conference in 1988. Every ten years all the bishops of the whole Anglican Communion throughout the world gather for a three-week conference. In 1988 it was held in Canterbury. Walking in procession into Canterbury Cathedral on that first Sunday morning, in the company of nearly six hundred other bishops, all of whom represented thousands if not millions of Christians from over one hundred and sixty countries, was an overwhelming experience which I shall never forget.

The awesome nature of that experience was reinforced the next day at the early morning service of Holy Communion when the bishops and their wives were gathered for worship. Nearly twelve hundred people joined in saying the Christian family prayer 'Our Father . . .' with each person present saying the prayer in his or her own language. The feeling of belonging to a universal family was intense, real and very enriching.

But that part of the world-wide Family which I encountered at the Lambeth Conference was only the Anglican part of it and, therefore, only a fraction of the whole. Across the world there are a multitude of Catholic, Protestant and Orthodox Christians – a truly multinational and multicultural Family. Those of us who live in Britain can tend to be a little blinkered when it comes to thinking of the Church of God. We can so easily fall into the trap of believing that the centre of the Christian world is to be found in this country and particularly in our parish or fellowship group. It can come as a great shock, to those of us who live in the somewhat sober and predictable ecclesiastical environment of Great Britain, to realise that in other parts of the world the Church and Family of God is vibrant with life and growing at a phenomenal rate.

### . . . *Stretching back into history*

Yet, to speak of the Family of God as spread across the whole world is also only part of the picture. It is to view the scene through a very small window. The full vision can only come into view when we see the Family of God as stretching back across history. During the course of one week in this past year I have had the pleasure of visiting five of the church buildings in my diocese to celebrate the anniversary of the dedication of each of them by my predecessor one hundred and fifty years ago. He obviously left his palace in Ripon – no doubt in a horse-drawn carriage – and did a 'job lot' while he was about it! But as I followed in his wake a century and a half later I was very moved by the fact that we were both part of the same Family. Indeed, as I move around my diocese taking thanksgiving services for churches built five hundred, a thousand, and in one case, thirteen hundred years ago, I am made very conscious of the Family of God stretching back across history. First and twentieth century disciples are part of the same Community of Faith. They are members of the same Family.

### . . . *You'll never walk alone*

The reason for beginning this chapter about the Church in this way was to get across to my readers two particularly important truths. The first is that in the Bible the word 'Church' doesn't refer to a building – as it so often does today – but to a body of people who share a common faith in Jesus Christ. The second is that the followers of that same Jesus do not commit themselves to a kind of 'oddball' existence which pursues individual piety in isolation from 'normal' people. On the contrary those who follow Jesus become part of a Family whose members are innumerable.

The first thing that Jesus did when he began his work on earth was to create a community. When he called people then, it was not to isolation nor to individualism but into a community. The same is true today. His call is a call to belong to a Family. No one has put this truth more helpfully or graphically than my beloved predecessor Geoffrey Paul when he said, 'Being a Christian is a matter of belonging to Christ with those who are his, and of course there is no way of belonging to Christ except by belonging gladly and irrevocably to all that marvellous and extraordinary ragbag of saints and fatheads who make up the one, holy, catholic and apostolic Church.'

Those who experience the companionship of Jesus also discover that they are in the company of a multitude which no man can number – across the world and across the ages.


PILGRIMS OF THE WAY . . .

One of the earliest names given to Christianity was *the Way*. It is a lovely and significant name implying, among other things, that the Christian life is a pilgrimage or a journey. It was Monica Furlong who described the religious person as 'one who believes that life is about making a journey' while the non-religious person is one who believes there is no journey to take. It is a good description of the Church or Family of God. Every individual member will be at a different stage of development – as is the case of the normal earthly family – but all are pilgrims on the same journey. It is a journey of faith. It is a journey towards God and towards the realisation of God's ultimate purpose for us. It is a pilgrimage on which only the extremely arrogant or naive would claim to have 'arrived'.

St Paul was no fool. He was an enthusiastic pilgrim on the journey. He was fully committed to reaching the journey's end and achieving the goal of God's ultimate purpose for him. Yet with commendable realism he declared:

> Not that I have . . . yet reached my goal, but I am still pursuing it in the attempt to take hold of the prize for which Christ Jesus took hold of me. Brothers, I do not reckon myself as having taken hold of it; I can only say that forgetting all that lies behind me, and straining forward to what lies in front, I am racing towards the finishing-point to win the prize of God's heavenly call in Christ Jesus.
>
> Philippians 3:12–14

Paul had the wisdom, or the common sense, to know that no one person could grasp the incomprehensible majesty of Christ in a single lifetime. The Christian having encountered or been encountered by Christ is on a pilgrim journey of discovery. He or she, and indeed the whole Church, has not yet arrived. Like British Rail we are 'getting there' but we have not yet reached our destination.

### . . . The starting-point

Some people can recall a specific point at which they began their journey of faith. Others can't be quite so certain while many simply can't remember a time when they were not Christian pilgrims. I am one of those who can point to a time and place when I 'encountered' or 'was encountered by' Christ. I was nineteen at the time and my 'conversion' experience could be said to mark the beginning of my journey. However, there is great wisdom in some words of the theologian Kierkegaard, 'Life is lived looking forward . . . but understood looking backward.' The truth of his words came home to me in a somewhat unusual manner.

Immediately after my ordination in 1963 I travelled to Belfast and preached my very first sermon in my home church of St Donard's. Now for those newly ordained there is a great temptation to see themselves as God's gift to the Church and at the time I don't think I had entirely conquered that particular temptation! Certainly I intended telling the large congregation that despite my baptism and confirmation in that very same church my journey did not begin until the night of my 'conversion', again in that same church. But as I climbed the steps into the pulpit I was overcome by what I can only describe as the conviction of the Holy Spirit that my perception was wrong and my understanding somewhat superficial. I suddenly saw that it was not despite my baptism and confirmation but *because* of them that I was enabled to enter into the experience of conversion to Christ.


*. . . Baptism*

In the sacrament of baptism God had drawn near to me in love and acceptance even though I was unaware of it at the time. Within the family of the church and through its nurture and care God had continued patiently to express his love for me until I reached the point of my life when I was able to see the wonder of it for the first time and respond to it. Living my life looking forward I saw the 'conversion' experience as the beginning of my journey of faith. But looking backward I came to understand, what I couldn't grasp at the time, that God had been journeying with me from the moment of my baptism – and perhaps before!

Within the universal Church or Family of God baptism is viewed as the official starting-point of the journey of faith. Indeed in the New Testament, becoming a Christian and being baptised are virtually synonymous. Baptism is taken for granted. No sooner were individuals or families converted than they were baptised (see Acts 2:38, 41, 47). It was the initiation rite into the Family of God. It was the way of admitting new members – and so it remains. Of course, on the matter of infant baptism, Churches hold different viewpoints, each with its own strengths and weaknesses. Nevertheless, baptism is the mark of the Christian Community. It signifies that we have come to Christ, that we have forsaken our selfish ways, that we have been forgiven and renewed and have become the children of God. As Paul put it, '. . . all of you are the children of God, through faith, in Christ Jesus, since every one of you that has been baptised has been clothed in Christ' (Galatians 3:26–7).


*. . . No opting out*

When Bishop Azariah of North India baptised new converts in the local river he always involved them in a simple yet significant piece of symbolism. As the newly baptised came up out of the water they were invited to place their hands on their heads and say, with the Bishop, these words from 1 Corinthians 9:16, 'Woe to me if I do not preach the gospel!' By that simple action he impressed upon them the fundamental truth that baptism into Christ involves us willy-nilly in the mission of Christ. At baptism we cease to be spectators and become involved in the action.

In the journey of faith – as in every other walk of life –

privilege is accompanied by responsibility. When Jesus was baptised, as we saw in chapter 3, he received all the reassurance that baptism can bring. He was reminded of the privilege of acceptance and Sonship. He was made aware of the strengthening presence of the Holy Spirit. But immediately he was baptised he was thrust, quite literally, by that same Spirit into the wilderness to endure the testing experience of hardship and doubt. In other words the privilege of being God's Son carried with it the responsibility of getting on with the job. There was no opting out. His baptism marked the inauguration of his ministry and mission – the beginning of his service of love and compassion towards the world.

*. . . Called to serve*

It cannot be different for those who today follow him in the Way. As a consequence of their baptism they are required to get on with the job of being Christ's disciples. Indeed their baptism is really their public commissioning to serve the world in the name of Christ. By the manner of their service to others they are to demonstrate the reality of Christ's love for the world of today. This is nowhere better expressed than in some words from Matthew's Gospel:

'Lord, when did we see you hungry and feed you, or thirsty and give you drink? When did we see you a stranger and make you welcome, lacking clothes and clothe you? When did we find you sick or in prison and go to see you?' And the King will answer, 'In truth I tell you, in so far as you did this to one of the least of these brothers of mine, you did it to me.'

Matthew 25:37–40

Disciples of Jesus are called to serve not only those who are members of the Church, but also those who many consider to be outside the Church but very much within the love and concern of God.

### . . . *Food for the journey*

Marathon races are now commonplace throughout the world. The most famous in this country is the London Marathon in which over thirty thousand runners take part. Many of them run not just for personal prestige but in order to bring sponsored financial help to needy charities. One of the fascinating features of the race over the years has been the development of helpful methods of providing necessary nourishment for the runners during the race.

God similarly has provided the Church with the necessary 'nourishment' to sustain Christian pilgrims on their journey of faith. That sustenance can take many forms, including the wonders of the universe, the beauty of this world in which we live, the variety of its creatures, the works of science and art, and above all the gift of mutual love which reflects the likeness of God himself. But one particular provision of God for his Church is to be found in the Eucharist (also called Holy Communion, the Lord's Supper or the Mass). The Eucharist (which means Thanksgiving) is one of the two principal sacraments of the Church. The other is baptism. A sacrament is the outward and visible sign of an inward and spiritual grace given to us by Christ himself. He gave us baptism to unite us with Christ, to receive his forgiveness and to mark the beginning of our journey with him. He gave us the Eucharist as our 'food' for that journey because in the Eucharist the focus is on Jesus – especially on his death and resurrection.

It was on the night before he died that Jesus instituted

the Eucharist and gave it to the Church not only as a memorial of him but also as a means of grace and a source of spiritual sustenance for them: 'Then he took bread, and when he had given thanks, he broke it and gave it to them, saying, "This is my body given for you; do this in remembrance of me." He did the same with the cup after supper, and said, "This cup is the new covenant in my blood poured out for you" ' (Luke 22:19–20).

## . . . *Risen but not recognised*

Though the Eucharist is a central feature in the life and worship of the Church it has also been a focus of controversy with some Churches placing great emphasis upon it and others almost ignoring it. Such controversy need not delay us here. There is perhaps greater agreement on the significance of the Eucharist today than at any other stage in the Church's history. Perhaps the little incident in the village of Emmaus on the night following the resurrection of Jesus gives us the classic understanding of its meaning for today. The Risen Jesus having walked with two of his followers from Jerusalem to Emmaus accepted their invitation to stay and have supper with them because dusk was falling. Throughout the whole of that journey of about seven miles they had failed to recognise him. But at supper, 'they had recognised him at the breaking of the bread' (Luke 24:35).

That same 'recognition' is the regular experience of those who are pilgrims on the journey of faith today. As they meet for worship and fellowship at the Eucharist they are conscious of the presence of the Risen Lord with them and they are spiritually fed by that presence. The two earthly elements of bread and wine are invested with all the significance of what they represent in terms of Christ's love and sacrifice for us. As Christian pilgrims stretch out empty hands to receive these tangible signs of God's love for them they are all too conscious of being given food for the journey. Baptism is received once for it marks the start of our pilgrimage. The Eucharist is received regularly because it is necessary nourishment as the journey progresses. Indeed it is the foretaste of the feast that will mark the end of the journey and the completion of God's ultimate purpose for us.

RELUCTANT PILGRIMS . . .

I spend rather a lot of my time going to church. Frequently, while waiting to be 'wheeled on' to do my bishop 'bit', I am placed on a special seat at the 'top end' of the church, where I sit in splendid isolation, in danger of becoming more of a spectator than a participant. Quite often at such times I ask myself a probing question, 'If I didn't have to come to this church, would I do so by choice?' On occasions the answer is even more painful than the question! To be honest much of what is going on seems to be irrelevant as far as the world outside is concerned and, if I wasn't already a Christian pilgrim, I would need some convincing as to why I should become one – if it means joining the local church.

At the same time, my task as bishop inevitably involves me in many aspects of the life of society which lie outside the institutional Church. This means that I have to live with contradictions. One such contradiction is that there are those in society who sit very loosely to the Church as an institution but who, nevertheless, reveal many of the characteristics of a pilgrim on the journey of faith. Their commitment to what I believe to be the teaching of Jesus, together with their compassionate care of the needy, leaves me with little doubt that they share the same journey as I do.

It is not that they are antagonistic towards the Church. The opposite is frequently true. They want to belong. They feel that the Church is meant to express the loving generous nature of the God whom they sense to be real. But they genuinely find it difficult to make the connection between the practical and compassionate love of Jesus and the manner in which the institutional Church expresses it. The Church's apparent concern with the maintenance of its own life while it claims to follow a Lord who laid down his life for the sake of others is a major contradiction which seems hard to resolve. As is its apparent incompetence in communicating its gospel to the poor and its spiritual poverty in a secular age. Only those Christians who wear rose-coloured spectacles would fail to see that the Church is far from being the kind of community which God intended. There is no avoiding the fact that the institutional Church is humiliated by its failure to be what it professes to be or what it is told to be.

A SCHOOL FOR SINNERS . . .

But we should not be surprised that the Church is not a perfect community. It is a pilgrim community of imperfect sinful people who, with God's help, are grappling with the life of faith on their journey through a complex and perplexing world. By definition, as we have seen, pilgrims are those who have not yet 'arrived'. They struggle with the hardness of the way as well as with their own personality weaknesses. The same is true of the term 'disciple'. A disciple is not one who knows it all, but one who is in the process of learning. In ordinary life we learn by our mistakes. The Christian life is no different. The Church is not a club for the perfect but a school for sinners. Jesus made this abundantly clear on one occasion when he was severely criticised for keeping company with sinners:

> In his honour Levi held a great reception in his house, and with them at table was a large gathering of tax collectors and others. The Pharisees and their scribes complained to his disciples and said, 'Why do you eat and drink with tax collectors and sinners?' Jesus said to them in reply, 'It is not those who are well who need the doctor, but the sick. I have come to call not the upright but sinners to repentance.'
>
> Luke 5:29–32

Every Sunday as the followers of Jesus meet for worship they receive from God a fresh call to repentance (to turn from sin to God). For, though pilgrims on the journey of faith they remain sinners in need of forgiveness and renewal for the way ahead.

THE GIFT OF GOD . . .

Alongside the contradictions that surround the life of the Church in the world we must place the redeeming truth – that the Church is the gift of God. Despite its weakness, its compromise, its sin and its shortcomings, it is the gift of God – 'a wonderful and sacred mystery' for which Jesus gave his life (Ephesians 5:27). It is his gift placed within the world for the sake of the world's salvation, that is, to set the world free from every kind of fear.

When Jesus taught his disciples to pray 'Thy Kingdom come' he was giving them a vision of, and asking them to pray and work towards, a time when God's will would be done on earth as it is in heaven. A time when justice, righteousness, peace and love would fill the whole earth. But Jesus was also a realist. He taught that such a Kingdom would not come overnight. Its arrival would be gradual and would be accompanied by much hardship, conflict and suffering. Until the day when it had arrived in all its fullness there would always be a struggle between good and evil, between the perfect and the imperfect.

Since the Church is placed in the world with the specific purpose of helping to bring in that Kingdom it is not at all surprising that the Church should contain within itself much of the pain and perplexity, as well as some of the promise and potential of the Kingdom. God has placed his Church in the world not to avoid this conflict but in order to redeem it. Christ is the world's true Redeemer but he brings his redeeming love within sight and reach of the world through the compassionate and loving (if imperfect) service of his Church. The Church is the servant of the world.

The Church, then, is a pilgrim people held by a common vision – the coming of the Kingdom of God in all its fullness. The Church is a pilgrim people committed to a common task – the sharing of the Good News of God's love. The Church is a pilgrim people across the world and across the ages – sharing the journey of faith in the company of its Risen Lord.

## Questions

1. Many people believe that our journey doesn't really begin until we can point to a starting-point e.g. like conversion. Do you agree?
2. Many devout people of other faiths believe themselves to be on a journey towards God. Do you think it may

71

turn out to be the same journey that is being made by Christians?

3. How would you set out to convince a reasonably sympathetic listener that it is a good thing to join the Church?

4. Can you explain why it is that some people who don't align themselves with any particular church or faith nevertheless live better lives than some of those who do?

5. Is it possible to love God and yet have no practical concern for his needy children at home or overseas?

# 6

# Light for the Journey
## *The use of the Bible to guide us*

We all like to receive presents, especially if they come as a surprise, like the one I was given by some friends when I was leaving Nottingham to become Bishop of Bradford. It was very securely and attractively wrapped and at first I thought it was the customary clock – but it seemed a little too bulky for that. I then imagined it might be a radio – though it felt rather heavy for that.

In the end I satisfied my curiosity and brought pleasure to my friends by unwrapping the paper to uncover a pair of sturdy walking boots. It marked the start of a new hobby for me; hill-walking amongst the famous and very beautiful Yorkshire Dales. Since then I have acquired all the other equipment considered necessary for the hill-walker. Maps, thumb-sticks, rucksacks and a spare pair of boots have all become part of my 'stock-in-trade'. All of it specially chosen to help meet the challenges and conditions one encounters on a journey through the lovely Dales and Fells of this part of the world.

In a similar way God has offered us various 'helps' as we travel through life on a journey of faith. We have already mentioned some of them in earlier chapters of this book. There is the supreme help of the companionship of Jesus made possible by the Holy Spirit. But there is also a great variety of other resources to guide and assist us towards the successful completion of the journey. These include prayer and the sacraments, as well as the love and example of other people, together with the mystery and beauty of God's creation. But there is one particular source of inspiration and help which has brought light and guidance to Christian pilgrims across the ages and that is the Bible, the word of God, the Holy Scriptures. The writer of Psalm 119 likens the word of God to a torch shining on a dark night and helping the traveller to walk safely on his journey. Though he is giving a personal testimony in a specific set of circumstances his words sum up the experience of Christian pilgrims the world over, 'Your word is a lamp for my feet, a light on my path'.


A LAMP AND A LIGHT . . .

When the psalmist speaks of the word of God being like a lamp and a light to guide us we need to be as clear as possible about what he means. He was referring specifically to the first five books of the Bible known as the Torah, or the Law. The Torah was, as it were, God's torch for the darkness. It was his guidance and direction for his people on their pilgrim journey. The writer of Psalm 119 (v. 105) wasn't inferring that God's word would provide simple and unmistakable guidance for every aspect of our daily life or chosen career. Rather he was teaching that just as a torch throws light on a dark path and helps us to avoid the otherwise unseen pitfalls, so God's word helps to cast light on those difficult moral choices that are inevitable as we journey through a complex world.

One of the things which Jesus did was to take the Old Testament (including Psalms) and fill out its meaning with a contemporary significance and application. An illustration of this is to be seen in the record of the temptations of Jesus contained in Matthew's Gospel. As I mentioned in chapter 3, it seems that the real point of that threefold temptation was to face Jesus with a moral dilemma, 'Does the end justify the means?' On each of the three occasions he was tempted he recalled the Scriptures, the written word of God, and allowed them to throw light on the darkness of the moral dilemma. Three times he replies, 'Scripture says' (see Matthew 4:4, 6 and 7) and he made his decision in the light of it. In other words the word of God was a lamp to his feet and a light to his path. It helped him make the right moral choice.

Jesus held a high view of Scripture and the Church has followed his example. What the writer of Psalm 119 claimed for the Law or Torah, as contained in the first five books of the Bible, the Church of God claims for the whole Bible. It is a lamp containing God's light for his children on their pilgrimage through the darkness of this world.

## . . . Not an idol

It is because I share the high esteem for the Bible, as held by Jesus and the universal Church, that I get anxious about some attitudes towards it that seem to drag it down to the level of unreality and ridicule.

One of the most memorable experiences of life in Bradford was the visit my wife and I made to a small, independent school for Muslim girls between the ages of thirteen and sixteen. The courtesy and sensitivity of the girls were most impressive as were the academic ability and commitment of their teachers. As a result of that experience two particular memories remain with me. The first was the question time when the girls, having graciously asked my permission to do so, put to me some very intelligent, enlightening and at times very challenging questions. I wonder what my readers would have answered if they had been asked, 'What would you do if your son became a Muslim?' The second memory that stands out for me was the suitably inscribed gift of a rather beautiful copy of the Koran. I learned from the head teacher that such was the Muslim reverence for their Holy Book that nothing must be placed on top of it – thus relegating it to a lower level. Indeed it ought not to be inconspicuously placed at a lower level than other items in a room. Now this is a tradition which though I don't share I nevertheless respect.

Within the Christian tradition there is a quite proper reverence for the Bible. But there are some who appear to take this reverence to an extreme not far short of idolatry. While I respect the motives of such people I cannot share their attitude. The Bible, they imply, must not be questioned. Nor can any criticism of it be allowed. Since it is God's word it must be infallible, which usually means totally accurate in all that it says on any subject. Apparently no allowance is made for the fact that two people, each of whom may hold the Scriptures in high esteem, can come to totally opposite conclusions about what a particular part of it means.

But the Bible must be seen as a lamp to guide rather than an idol to be worshipped. When a book, albeit one as important and unique as the Bible, is given the kind of status and reverence which should be reserved for the Lord himself, we are treading on rather dangerous ground. The central doctrine of the Christian religion is that of the incarnation – God became a human being. But it is important to remember that he became incarnate in a life, the life of Jesus, and not in a book.

*. . . Nor a lucky dip*

Summer fêtes and Christmas fairs are regular features of community life. Their purpose is usually to provide funds for worthwhile charities. One of the most popular features of such community events, especially for children, is the bran tub. Small, usually heavily-wrapped, gifts are placed in a tub of sawdust or wood-chippings. Quite literally, 'You pay your money and you take your pick!' Having handed over the required amount you are permitted to rummage around in the tub and come up with one of the hidden gifts. It may or may not match the money you paid for the privilege, but it matters little since it's all for a good cause.

There are those who have a tendency to treat the Bible in the same way – though they wouldn't dream of behaving in that way towards any other book. It is viewed as a kind of religious bran tub. You simply dip into it and pick out whatever you fancy and apply it to your present circumstances. I remember doing this unashamedly as a young Christian. Sometimes it worked – and the verse I picked out seemed to match my mood or my circumstances perfectly. Sometimes it led to great confusion – as most things do when taken out of context. God on occasions graciously overlooked my naivety and used my 'lucky dip' method to bring me help from his word in the Bible. However, on mature reflection, I think it was an unworthy way in which to treat the Scriptures.

Perhaps these somewhat negative attitudes towards the Bible have been overstated but I have done so with a worthy purpose. I consider the value and authority of Scripture to be such that I don't wish to see them undermined by an unworthy approach to them. Too often sincere enquirers are put off by being made to feel that they must believe the Bible in a certain way. Many, in all integrity, cannot accept such a view. They therefore are made to feel guilty because their faith in God's word appears defective. This is not only a tragedy, it is also a travesty of the truth. God nowhere demands that we sacrifice our intellectual integrity in order to believe. We mustn't claim more for the Bible than it claims for itself. At the same time we must beware of attempts to belittle its power and influence. It is the supreme source document of Christianity. It therefore requires our respect, honesty, and willingness to respond to its unique story of God.

## A  LIBRARY . . .

Long before I became a committed follower of Jesus Christ I felt it would be a useful exercise to read through the Bible. Naturally I started at the book of Genesis and hopefully began the long journey towards the Revelation of St John. It was relatively easygoing at first. The story was interesting and the issues being dealt with had a basic human appeal. However, when I got to the books of Leviticus and Numbers I was not only way out of my depth but bored out of my mind. Shopping lists, inventories and family trees weren't exactly gripping stuff for a teenager, and so I called it a day.

It might have helped if, before I started, someone had explained that the Bible was a very complex book written by many hands, using three different languages, over a period of some eighteen hundred years. Far from being a single volume it was a library containing different types of literature. Among its sixty-six books are to be found history and narrative, poetry and prose, proverb and prophecy. Small wonder I found it such hardgoing. My approach to it was totally lacking in understanding.

What a difference it made when I learned to approach each type of literature in the Bible in the proper manner and with the right kind of expectation. Suddenly, for instance, the book of Psalms began to prove a real source of practical inspiration and comfort. I discovered that they were ancient hymns and poems whose colourful and symbolic language was not always meant to be taken literally. Yet, because they expressed in personal terms a man's experience of life and of God, they articulated some of my own inner feelings. They found an echo in my own life and experience of God.

### . . . Of human documents

No one would be more surprised than the writers of the Psalms to discover that their words – sometimes hymns of praise and at other times poems of complaint directed towards God – were now classified as 'the word of God'. As far as they were concerned they were speaking in very personal terms within a situation characterised above all by great humanness. But that fact simply highlights a truth which must never be forgotten in our attempts to understand the Bible. It is a collection of very human documents. Both the Old and the New Testaments were written in the ordinary languages of the day by ordinary human beings. When Paul wrote to Timothy (2 Timothy 3:16) that 'All scripture is inspired by God . . .' he certainly didn't intend to imply that the writers were sitting with their pens poised waiting to be told, via a heavenly public-address system, what they were to write.

On the contrary they were motivated by very human considerations. Dr John Goldingay illustrates the point superbly:

> It [the Bible] was written out of human motivation: Luke, for instance, tells us that he wrote a gospel because he thought it was a good idea (Luke 1:1–4). The Bible was written by ordinary human processes: thus Paul found, as letter-writers sometimes do, that he was not so sure later in one of his paragraphs that what he

had written earlier in that paragraph was quite right (see 1 Corinthians 1:14–16).

It is difficult to read the Scriptures without recognising, and honestly acknowledging, that the diverse personalities of the authors come through loud and clear.

### . . . But of more than human significance

In my introduction I told the story of the fairly intelligent and somewhat forthright teenager who asked me the question, 'Sir, was that true – or was it preaching?' Apparently he had been influenced by something I had said in my sermon and behind his somewhat precocious question was a more fundamental enquiry. Had he been moved simply by the power of oratory or had it been the truth of God which had affected him so deeply? It is a little incident to which I have returned again and again over the years as I have grown to know, love and, in a measure, understand the Bible. As I have said, it is a truly human document but, clearly, it is a document with more than human significance. It is not simply impressive oratory, fine prose or beautiful poetry. It is not merely the words of men and women. It speaks about God but it also speaks from God. As John Goldingay says, 'It is a book which has God behind it, a book which speaks of God's involvement in human history and carries illumination and challenge from God within its pages.'

This has been the corporate witness of the Church and the constant testimony of individuals throughout the ages. The Church came to accept these human documents as God's word because it recognised that they had an authenticity and an authority that were self-evident. That they clearly had God behind them was a conviction confirmed in the experience of individuals and communities. Written by human beings they, nevertheless, were human beings moved or inspired by God's Holy Spirit (2 Peter 1:21 and 2 Timothy 3:16). That same Spirit illuminates our minds today and helps us to understand what they wrote and to appreciate its contemporary relevance, power and influence. In the last analysis my respect for the Bible and my sincerely held conviction that it speaks from God are based on personal experience. It is not just the very positive attitude of Jesus towards the Scriptures nor the teaching and tradition of the Church that lead me to this conviction. My own life and ministry have been formed, and continue to be reformed, by the Scriptures. They are a constant lamp for my feet and light on my path as I journey on my Christian pilgrimage.


A STORY . . .


In experiencing light and guidance from the Scriptures it is not a question of the Bible being a kind of 'How to do it' book containing infallible blueprints of guidance for every conceivable situation. Rather it is much more a 'How God did it' book. It is a book which tells a story. It contains a whole series of stories but they all contribute to the one main story – the story of God's dealings with people and nations in historical situations.

Basically the Bible is the story of one people's journey with God and it has its focus in the person of Jesus Christ. It is a story which began before the world was created and which will end only when God draws all things to himself. It is the story of Abraham, and a journey into the unknown. It is the story of Moses and a journey from obscurity and captivity to leadership and liberation. It is the story of Job and his painful journey and perplexing struggle to make sense out of misfortune. It is the story of Paul and his journey through religious legalism, bigotry and prejudice to a change of character and a transformation of life from persecutor to preacher. It is supremely a story about God's Son, Jesus Christ, who comes from God as his Light for the world; perfectly revealing God's love and perfectly fulfilling God's will to rescue humanity from fear of every kind.

### . . . Like a window that opens

When my family were very young the children's television programme that captivated their attention – and gave their mother a brief respite each morning and afternoon – was called *Playschool*. One of the fascinating features of that lovely programme was a house with four windows each of a different shape. Each day during the programme the camera would focus through a different window and, in story form, open up for the young watchers some of the wonders of their world.

. The Bible is a story which opens up a window and allows us to see God's dealings with individuals, with groups of people and with nations. The light from that open window helps to guide us on the journey through our particular world. Through that window, for instance, and in the contents of that story we see God revealed as one who has an intense desire for justice, peace and reconciliation. In his dealings with people and nations he shows his deep concern for the integrity of creation. Men and women are not only the recipients of creation's privileges, they are also the stewards of its riches and are required to behave responsibly towards it. There are moving stories of a God who, though he on occasions hides himself, never abandons his people. He calls people to account for their selfishness, pride and their harsh treatment of the underprivileged. He is outspoken about those who in their folly worship gods who are impotent and he is forthright in his condemnation of religious people whose worship is full of ritual but empty of reality.

Above all, the compassionate love of God for all people is clearly and unmistakably revealed in the person of Jesus Christ. He is God's visible and living Word, that is, he is the fullest expression of what God is and thinks and does. As the story of Jesus unfolds in the Scriptures, as we watch his immense care for people, his willingness to serve others rather than be served and his refusal to save himself at the expense of his enemies, the window through which we are looking is filled with light. It has become a window not only onto the world and God's dealings with it, it also has become a window into the very heart of God himself.

## . . . Like a mirror that reflects

At the very beginning of my work as Bishop of Bradford I had the privilege of visiting every clergyperson in my diocese together with some of the leading layworkers.

Among other things I was trying to discover what made them tick as Christian disciples and as church leaders. What was the bedrock upon which their spirituality was based and by which their life of service to God and the community was sustained? Of course there was a considerable variety of detail in the answers I received but there was also a remarkable consensus. All without exception saw the reading and the study of the Holy Scriptures as a vital ingredient in the development of their Christian life and ministry.

I was impressed by this information but not in the least surprised. Far from being an 'other-worldly' occupation the study of the Scriptures produces a remarkable insight into how things really are in this present world. It is a

mirror in which reality is reflected. The closer I get to the
Scriptures the more I find myself in them. I can identify
myself in the individual stories. My hopes and aspirations,
my fears and my doubts are all portrayed in its pages.
Nowhere is this more true than in my daily reading of the
Psalms. Within those ancient hymns and poems, far from
finding escape from the real world, I discover a remarkable
insight into that world and my place within it. I am
reminded, for instance, that the two poles of human existence never alter. As the writer of Ecclesiastes says, 'there
is a time to weep and a time to laugh'. Within the Psalms
and, indeed, within so many other books and stories of
the Bible, I find words which accurately articulate my own
feelings and experiences of these two great realities of life.

But I not only find myself and the world in which I live
reflected in the Scriptures, I also find the pilgrim people
of God with whom I journey on the life of faith. I see God
dealing with people just like me and I see them struggling
with the same basic temptations and challenges that confront me. And, perhaps, most remarkable of all, I discover
that I am part of the same story as Abraham, Moses and
Job, as Paul, Peter and Andrew. The story is not only
God's story, it is my story. It's the story of the human
family to which I belong. It's the story of the world – the
home in which I live. It is the story of all those who, like
me, look for light and guidance on our journey through
life.

A BOOK FOR ALL HUMANITY . . .

But the Bible is not a trick mirror which reflects only
selected images. It is not an élitist book for an élitist group
of people. It is not the private property of Christians.
Indeed, some Christians can so easily forget that Jesus

was a Jew and that the Old Testament, which forms the larger portion of the Bible, emerged from the Hebrew tradition and environment. The coming of Christ didn't abolish the Old Testament. It simply filled it out and endorsed the character and purpose of God as portrayed by it. This should help us to understand that the Bible is not just a book for Christians. Nor is it just a book for private devotion or a textbook for sermons. *It is a book for all humanity*. Lord Blanch, a biblical scholar and former Archbishop of York, put it like this:

> The Bible is not just of the Church or for the Church. With one or two substantial exceptions, it portrays little interest in ecclesiastical affairs and concerns itself rather with the struggles, the tragedies, the aspirations and destiny of humanity itself. It is this which has given it a strange contemporaneity with centuries and cultures so different from the one within which it arose.

It is this quality of universal application and contemporary relevance which enables the Bible to be a light for the journey of all humankind. If we have eyes to see and ears to hear, Scripture is truly a lamp for our feet and a light on our path.

## Questions

1. Can you think of at least one incident or stage in your life when the Bible 'spoke' to you?
2. Just what kind of guidance ought I expect from the pages of the Bible in the living out of my life in today's world?
3. Am I lacking in faith if I do not believe every word of the Bible to be true?

4. Given that the Bible is really a library of books, are some more important than others?
5. Why do you think the Bible, despite its age and the context in which it was written, remains so remarkably contemporary?

# 7

## It Isn't All Sunshine
### *Faith and doubt walk side by side*

When the Beatles wrote and sang their popular hit song, 'Eleanor Rigby', with the words 'Just look at all the lonely people, where do they all come from?' they were not just voicing an emotional lyric, they were addressing one of life's realities. Loneliness is a universal human experience. C. S. Lewis put it like this, 'We are born helpless. As soon as we are fully conscious we discover loneliness. We need others physically, emotionally, intellectually, we need them if we are to know anything, even ourselves.' But loneliness is not only a universal human reality, it is also a very painful experience. Those who have suffered the loneliness which frequently follows in the wake of bereavement, marriage breakdown or deteriorating health, will bear witness to this fact. Such loneliness, because it may be both publicly perceived and sympathetically understood, can produce a positive and supportive response. But among the many other types of loneliness there is one which, by its very nature, lies hidden and, therefore, frequently remains misunderstood and unrelieved.

### THE LONELINESS OF DOUBT . . .

This particular truth was brought home to me very power-fully one day during the time when I was vicar of a Mid-lands parish. The telephone rang in my study early one evening. The call was from one of my leading lay people, a person for whom I had the highest regard and whose Christian life was exemplary. Indeed he was a constant source of help and encouragement to me and to many others in the church and local community. On this occasion his normally cheerful voice sounded rather muted and, sensing that something was wrong, I agreed to his request that he come and see me immediately. While I waited for him to arrive I went over in my mind the various things which might be the cause of his trouble. I went through a whole gamut of possibilities – redun-dancy, marriage problems, illness, all of which proved to be widely off the mark. For no sooner had he arrived at my home and been shown into my study than he rather nervously, and somewhat tearfully, said, 'Vicar, I think I have lost my faith.'

Now the story of that particular incident is rather long and somewhat involved and there is neither need nor space to record it in detail. But the crux of the matter was he was not losing his faith. He simply had hidden for years the fact that he had genuine doubts about certain aspects of the Christian faith as he had been taught it. Because everyone else in his local church – including the vicar – seemed to be free from doubts, he had kept his firmly under wraps. He had lived with the loneliness of doubt. The crunch had come when a rather unwise visit-ing preacher had suggested that faith and doubt were mutually exclusive. He had put two and two together and made six. He had come entirely to the wrong conclusion that because he had doubts he therefore couldn't possibly be holding to the Faith.

## . . . *Unnecessary*

I felt sorry for him. The guilty conscience regarding doubt which he had developed and the lonely silence which he had felt forced to endure were both totally unnecessary. For anyone even to suggest that faith and doubt were mutually exclusive was not only a travesty of the truth but also an extremely cruel and dangerous untruth. Indeed, if my friend had not had the courage and the courtesy to come and talk honestly and openly with me it might all have ended in tragedy. Instead it proved to be a positive and creative turning-point in his life. As we talked, the nature and extent of his doubts became clear. It wasn't that he was determined to oppose Christian truth in any shape or form. He hadn't made a conscious decision not to have faith in God. On the contrary, he genuinely wanted to believe – but with integrity. This resulted in him refusing to accept without question certain statements about God which he found difficult to understand or which made no meaningful connection with life as he knew it.

Such integrity calls for commendation rather than condemnation. Authentic Christian teaching and tradition nowhere require us to suspend the proper use of our critical faculties when it comes to faith. If, as C. S. Lewis indicated, loneliness is part of the universal human experience, the same is probably true concerning doubt. Very many, if not most Christian people would find an echo of their own experience in the extremely honest answer of the father of the epileptic boy in Mark's Gospel. He longed for Jesus to heal his son and asked him:

'If you can do anything, have pity on us and help us.'
'If you can?' retorted Jesus. 'Everything is possible for
one who has faith.' At once the father of the boy cried
out, 'I have faith. Help my lack of faith!'

Mark 9:23–5

In other words the father publicly declared, despite the
great psychological and emotional pressure to 'please'
Jesus by professing a 'pure' faith in order that his son
would be cured, that though he had faith he was not
without doubt. His words carry all the conviction of authenticity and truth. In his case faith and doubt were not
mutually exclusive.

### . . . Unhealthy

My friend had allowed himself to be intimidated into
silence by the assured faith and belief that appeared to
surround him in his church fellowship. Everyone seemed
so certain about what they believed that he was made to
feel that his faith was rather substandard by comparison.
He was afraid to give voice to his reservations in case he
would 'rock the boat'. It wasn't that people were consciously unkind to him. They were just oblivious to his
needs. Their commitment to the Faith left no room for it
to be questioned and, as a consequence, he was frozen
into silence. But inadvertently they were depriving him
and themselves of the possibility of growth as persons, to
say nothing of their healthy development as Christian
disciples.

Now of course there are many Christian people and
others who go through life, as it were, on a 'wing and a
prayer'. They give the impression of not having a care in
the world nor a doubt or uncertainty on their minds.
Such people ought not to be despised or envied. Biological

factors may have as much to do with their sunny dispositions as their theological beliefs. But in every walk of life, and the Christian life is no exception, the wise and humble use of our critical faculties is to be encouraged. The constructive questioning of beliefs and the critical examination of those patterns of behaviour based on such beliefs ought not to be dismissed as lack of faith or loss of faith. So-called doubts of this kind, far from being unhealthy and exclusive of faith, are a sign of creative health. They can open the way for growth towards true maturity of faith and personhood.

## THE GREAT PARADOX . . .

If, as I have said, doubt is probably part and parcel of the universal human experience, it is important to consider why this is so. Why do faith and doubt so often walk hand in hand? Many of the major personalities of the Bible, particularly of the Old Testament, wrestled with this question and Christians in every age have struggled with it too.

### . . . Known yet hidden

The answer seems to lie within the character of God.

God is revealed in the Bible as the God who is knowable. Indeed he is described as the God who has chosen to make himself known, in creation, in Scripture and supremely in the person of Jesus Christ. 'Anyone who has seen me', said Jesus, 'has seen the Father' (John 14:9). But, at the same time, as Isaiah tells us and as so much of life's experiences confirm, God is also the one who hides himself. 'Truly, you are a God who conceals himself' (Isaiah 45:15).

Here, I believe, is the striking paradox which lies at the heart of the strange companionship between faith and doubt in human experience and few of us can escape from the tension of it. Of course, some find it uncomfortable to live with paradox. They prefer things to be neat, tidy and, if possible, pigeon-holed! But life is not like that. We are constantly being forced to live with paradox and the essence of paradox is that it must not be resolved. It holds together two truths which at first sight seem contradictory but which actually need to be held together if we are to see the complete picture. 'There are two sides of every coin' is a traditional way of expressing the essence of paradox. To talk of immanence and transcendence is a theological way of describing something of the paradox of God's character. But in my experience it is usually much simpler than that. There are times when God seems so close that I could reach out and touch him. At other times he seems so remote that I feel alone and out of touch with him. Nearness and distance, that is the paradox that many, even mature Christians, have to live with from day to day.

### . . . It isn't all sunshine

The title of this chapter was not chosen in order to be 'with it'. The title portrays the paradox. The sun never ceases to shine but frequently it is hidden behind clouds. Indeed, if like me you live in a place like Yorkshire, there are times in the depths of winter, when you might wonder if it will ever shine again! Many of the wonderful human characters whose stories are told in the Bible must on occasions have felt like that. People like Jacob, Moses, Jeremiah and the writers of the Psalms all had the experience of basking in the sunshine of faith. Times when things were going right for them, God was in his heaven and all was well with the world. But the Bible honestly records the other occasions when their experience seemed almost to deny the very existence of God. Times when they argued against his apparent injustices and doubted the extent of his care for them.

Even John the Baptist, whom Jesus described as 'the greatest' (Matthew 11:11), experienced doubt. The sunshine of faith had shone upon him at the height of his popularity when crowds flocked to hear him preach at the River Jordan. He was thrilled to fulfil his calling to point other people to Jesus. But when he was cast into prison because of his fearless stand against immorality the clouds of doubt began to hide the sun. In the depths of his loneliness he sent his former disciples to Jesus with this poignant question which, at the least, seemed to imply the devastating doubt that after all he might have got it wrong: 'Are you the one who is to come, or are we to expect someone else?' (Matthew 11:3)

John's questioning resulted in a greater assurance of faith. He had not been mistaken. The claims he had made about Jesus in preparing the way for him were being fully justified. This was the answer Jesus gave to John's question:

'Go back and tell John what you see and hear; the blind see again, and the lame walk, those suffering from virulent skin-diseases are cleansed, and the deaf hear, the dead are raised to life and the good news is proclaimed to the poor; and blessed is anyone who does not find me a cause of falling.'

John remained in prison. He died in prison – for his faith, which was not diminished but strengthened by his questioning doubt. John, perhaps, above all others would have appreciated the little prayer found written on a wall by a Jewish prisoner in Cologne during the war:

> I believe in the sun even when it is not shining
> I believe in love even when I cannot feel it
> I believe in God, even when he is silent.

## THE WAYS OF GOD . . .

An important part of my job is to understand people, including myself. To know a person's strengths and weaknesses is a necessary ingredient to people management. It can also be great fun predicting how certain individuals will react in any given circumstance. My friends tell me that, despite my cultivated efforts to hide it, they can recognise in my demeanour the signs of boredom. Apparently they can also predict when a temperamental explosion is imminent! My own family assure me that when people have overstayed their welcome in my home I have a tendency to whistle or hum when they are about to leave.

God is not so transparent. He is faithful and can be trusted. He keeps his word and fulfils his promise. Nevertheless, as the famous old hymn declares, 'God moves in a mysterious way his wonders to perform'. If the character of God, with its paradox of distance and nearness, is one of the reasons why faith and doubt walk hand in hand, then another is the ways of God, that is, the manner in which he works.

### . . . *River or canal?*

Many years ago, John Oman wrote a very fine book called *Grace and Personality* in which he used a piece of imagery which I have always found helpful in pondering the ways of God. He wrote, 'God does not conduct his rivers, like arrows, to the sea but allows them to wind about, to meander, in their journeying to the sea.' We mortals, especially of the late twentieth century, like to draw straight lines, find the shortest routes, and exalt economy of effort. Oman went on, 'The expedition of man's small power and short day produces the canal, but nature, with a beneficient and picturesque circulambulancy, produces the river.'

Oman's imagery provides us with a wonderful insight into the mysterious ways of God. God patiently pursues his purposes for us. Sometimes, like the river, they involve meandering through open meadows, surrounded by beauty and sunshine. At other times they require us, like the river, to pass through a narrow ravine where the waters are dark and turbulent. Frequently, in similar fashion to the river, they are deflected and forced to find another, perhaps more tortuous, route to the sea of our eventual destination.

Few of my readers, I feel sure, would fail to recognise their own experience of life in this imagery. Most of us would prefer to be like the canal, predictable, straight-forward with little possibility of taking a wrong turning. Instead, life is much more like the river, turning this way and that, sometimes in sunshine and sometimes in shadow. Sometimes meandering and peaceful, and at other times restless, pressurised, unpredictable and even dangerous. The possibilities for doubt on the canal can be relatively few. On the river they can be limitless – but so also can the possibilities for growth in faith and personality.

## THE COURAGE TO DOUBT . . .

This may seem a rather strange way to refer to something which is so often considered to be destructive. Doubt is rarely spoken of in positive terms. But what I have been trying to say is that if our doubt is neither blatant unbelief nor self-conscious scepticism, but a genuine questioning of accepted ideas in our search for truth, then it is creative rather than destructive. Without such enquiry and exploration growth towards the truth is likely to be impossible. But with such things we are likely to develop a faith which is strong, mature and durable, as in the case of John the Baptist.

Of course there are those who, like my lonely friend at the beginning of this chapter, are afraid to voice their doubts. There are others who are afraid not only to admit their doubts to others but also to themselves because they simply can't live with any kind of uncertainty – and especially uncertainty regarding their Christian faith. Perhaps some words of Bishop Richard Holloway of Edinburgh in one of his books will be as helpful to them as they have been to me:

The true medium and habitat of Faith is more like water than stone, and believing is more like floating than marching with hobnailed boots on. That analogy is not meant to downgrade Faith. After all, floating on ten thousand fathoms of water takes more courage than pounding round the parade ground of modern certainties.

One of the funniest and yet the most embarrassing moments that my wife and I can remember was supplied by our daughter when she was four years old. We were welcoming to our home someone whom we regarded very highly and whom we were, rather foolishly perhaps, hoping to impress. To our acute embarrassment our rather gushing doorstep welcome was interrupted by the penetrating words of our precocious, but honest, four-year-old. 'Do you know', she said to our visitor in a somewhat remonstrative tone, 'my mother has spent the whole morning cleaning the house for you coming?' We do ourselves no favours if we sweep our doubts under the carpet and pretend they don't exist, just as we do no favours to the faith of others if we engage in idle and unnecessary speculation about things in which they firmly believe. Integrity, honesty and openness are the best guarantee of a healthy and developing faith. Thomas had those characteristics in abundance.

### . . . Thomas – the one who was missing

It would be difficult to write this chapter regarding doubt and the life of faith without mentioning the one disciple of Jesus whose name is forever associated with doubt. Doubting Thomas has been the subject of sermons and discussions throughout the centuries. He has been the object of criticism and negative comment. People have been dubbed with his name as a sign of derision. But, personally, I think he is much maligned. Indeed, I would prefer to associate him with courage rather than doubt. Thomas was an inquisitive individual who was always searching for greater clarity of understanding. He considered the words of Jesus to be so unclear and confusing on one occasion that he pressed him to be more specific. 'You know the way to the place where I am going', said Jesus to his disciples, just before his death. The other disciples were afraid to confess their ignorance, but not Thomas. He said, 'Lord, we do not know where you are going, so how can we know the way?' It is very worthy of note that it was Thomas' open confession of ignorance and his forthright search for greater clarity that produced one of the greatest sayings and claims of Jesus:

I am the Way; I am Truth and Life.
No one can come to the Father except through me.
If you know me, you will know my Father too.
From this moment you know him and have seen him.

John 14:6–7

But Thomas was not only inquisitive, he was a very determined and courageous character. A 'grasper of nettles' if ever there was one. On one occasion, such was his determination and courage that he was prepared to die with Jesus (John 11:16). It was that determination and courage that caused him to express his doubt about the resurrection of Jesus, even in the face of his fully convinced fellow-disciples. The immortal story is told in St John's Gospel. On the evening of his resurrection Jesus had appeared to his disciples in the Upper Room. He showed them his hands and his side – the marks of death and, indeed, the evidence of the resurrection – and he gave them his peace. But Thomas was missing and, when the other disciples told him what had happened and how they had seen the Risen Jesus, he refused to believe them. Indeed, in characteristically determined fashion, he told them he would never believe until he could see for himself and place his hands into the wounds of Jesus, 'Unless I can see the holes that the nails made in his hands and can put my finger into the holes they made, and unless I can put my hand into his side, I refuse to believe.' Thomas was no gullible push-over when it came to faith!

*. . . Thomas – the one for whom Jesus came back*

One of the reasons why I particularly like the story of Thomas is the wonderfully gracious and understanding attitude of Jesus. I know myself well enough to say that if I had been faced with Thomas' vociferous and faithless attitude my response would have been, 'Tough, Thomas, you've missed your chance, now stew in it.' It is forever recorded, however, that Jesus came back for Thomas. Oh, he rebuked him for his lack of faith in refusing to believe what his fellow-disciples had told him. But, and this is so important, he also responded positively to Thomas' desire to believe by inviting him to discover faith in his resurrection. Standing for the second time in that Upper Room, only this time with Thomas present, he spoke to him, 'Put your finger here; look, here are my hands. Give me your hand; put it into my side. Do not be unbelieving any more, but believe' (John 20:24–9).

The crux of the story for me is the fact that Thomas' expression of faith became the greatest and most convinced of all the disciples. Confronted with the Risen Lord, all his questions were answered and he confessed, 'My Lord and my God.' His doubts sincerely held and, courageously, if vociferously, expressed had led him to the fullness and integrity of faith.


FAITH TO BELIEVE . . .

Rarely a week goes past without my hearing from the lips of those whom I am about to initiate and welcome into the Church through baptism and confirmation these words:

> I believe and trust in God the Father, who made the world. I believe and trust in his Son, Jesus Christ, who

redeemed mankind. I believe and trust in the Holy Spirit, who gives life to the people of God.

I hear this profession of faith from hundreds of people each year and it never ceases to thrill me. Like Thomas, when confronted by the living God, faith is the only fitting response. Even those great Bible characters who seemed to rebel against what others were confidently affirming about God, did so in order to retain true faith in God.

In the last analysis we can claim no credit for faith. It is a gift from God. Faith depends on Jesus from start to finish. It is he 'who leads us in our faith and brings it to perfection' (Hebrews 12:2). At its simplest, faith is taking God at his word. It is, perhaps, at its most difficult when there is no obvious word from God. It was Tennessee Williams who wrote, 'The speechlessness of God is a long, long terrible thing.' But when God is silent, it is then that so often faith matures. We learn to thank him when he is near and to trust him when he is distant. Faith is not always diminished by doubt nor is doubt always demolished by faith. They are not mutually exclusive.

A former colleague of mine perhaps got closest to the truth when he said, 'Faith is the capacity to live with doubt.' The father of the epileptic boy would surely agree. 'Lord, I have faith. Help my lack of faith.'

## Questions

1. Why is it that some Christians are reluctant to talk about genuine doubts which they may have regarding their faith?
2. 'Truly, you are a God who conceals himself' (Isaiah 45:15). What does this particular characteristic of God

mean and how would we expect to encounter it in our daily lives?

3.  Can you recall an occasion in your life when God's way for you seemed more like a river than a canal?

4.  Thomas has been called 'the patron saint of creative doubt'. Is there such a thing as creative doubt? If so, how would we expect to profit from it on our journey of faith?

5.  How would you explain faith to:
    (a) a seven-year-old;
    (b) a sixth-former;
    (c) a young couple with two small children?

# 8

# Yes – But!
## *The problem of suffering*

Andrew and Stephen were healthy six-year-olds. They lived opposite each other in the same road. They attended the same school, shared the same interests and, with their parents, went to the same church. They were great pals and on occasions seemed inseparable. Stephen is my son. He has grown up to have three sons of his own. Andrew died when he was seven as a result of a brain tumour.

I shall never forget the tragedy. I was a young assistant curate at the time, enjoying my work in a Sussex parish and feeling very sure of, and secure in, the love of God. But how was I to explain to myself, as well as Andrew's mother and father, why Andrew was 'taken' and Stephen was left? How was I to continue to talk and preach about the love of God when an innocent child was so suddenly and tragically removed from those who loved him so dearly? For weeks it was agony for me to enter my home, close the door and play with my own son while knowing that in the house just opposite Andrew's parents were bereft and desolate. To the love of God I had always been able to say a loud and sincere 'Yes'. *But*, at that particular moment in my life, the love of God did appear to be somewhat selective, if not downright unfair.

## A BARRIER TO BELIEF? . . .

That human story, which lies deeply embedded in my memory, illustrates one of the harsher realities of life. It also serves to pin-point one of the great universal barriers to belief in God. Certainly in all my experience of ministering to people over the years the one subject which comes to the surface again and again is the issue of suffering. However logically one might preach, however persuasively one might speak, however reasonably one might present the Christian faith, people have a problem with suffering. 'Yes,' they will say, 'we see the power and attractiveness of what you are saying – but, what about suffering?' 'Surely, if God is a loving God he will not allow the innocent to suffer. Is it not reasonable to believe that if God is as powerful as Christians say he is he will prevent or put an end to suffering?' So runs the natural response of many who see suffering as a problem. In the face of so much unresolved, and apparently undeserved, suffering how can Christians continue to claim that God is both loving and powerful?

### . . . A God who doesn't care?

In the face of such suffering many people feel themselves forced to the conclusion that God simply doesn't care. And certainly some of the tragedies of life, even within my own experience, could be superficially interpreted in such a way. I well remember feeling just like that when I heard the news that the wife of my blind friend had died. For years she had been not only the light of his life – but his eyes as well. Now suddenly that light was extinguished and, it seemed, the darkness was complete. What on earth was God playing at?

But if our individual memories can produce their own

vivid examples of God's apparent lack of care, what are we to make of those breath-taking, heart-rending scenes – by courtesy of our television screens – on the plains of Ethiopia and Sudan? Pot-bellied children, with emaciated limbs and staring eyes, without food and without hope, waiting for relief which, for many of them, will only come in the form of death. The cries of God's children rend the heart, assault the mind and challenge the faith – and sometimes God seems to be unavailable for comment. If we are honest, are there not times when we all feel like this? 'God has forsaken me. God has forgotten me. God has ceased to care.' Those are sentiments which even the friends of God have uttered in the face of suffering across the centuries.

### . . . A God who allocates pain and prizes?

'What have I done to deserve this?' is another and very common way of presenting the problem of suffering. But it is not just a twentieth century way of giving expression to the problem. It was put to Jesus in rather similar terms nearly two thousand years ago when, on his travels, he encountered a man who had been blind from birth. 'Rabbi,' asked his disciples, 'who sinned, this man or his parents, that he should have been born blind?' (John 9:2, 3) Jesus refuses to endorse their false assumption that there was a necessary connection between suffering and sin. 'Neither he nor his parents sinned,' he replied. He then went on to suggest that a proper attitude in the face of suffering was not tortuous questions about who was responsible but a genuine endeavour to remove it with the help of God.

Jesus was not prepared to go along with a commonly held view that suffering was the direct result of sin. It was not to be seen as punishment for sin, just as health and prosperity were not to be viewed as the inevitable outcome of a relatively blameless life. God does not distribute pain for sinners and prizes for saints. Indeed, the so-called problem only becomes a problem because the opposite is so often the case. Certainly this was what bothered the writer of Psalm 73. He couldn't understand why God allowed the wicked to prosper:

> They have no struggles;
>     their bodies are healthy and strong.
> They are free from the burdens common to man;
>     they are not plagued by human ills.

He went on to complain that there appeared to be 'no justice'. Since God didn't appear to notice that he had been trying his best to live an upright life, he wondered if it was worth the effort.

> Surely in vain have I kept my heart pure;
>     in vain have I washed my hands in innocence.
>                                 Psalm 73:4, 5, 13 (NIV)

The psalmist puts his finger on the spot. It is undeserved suffering that really rends the heart, troubles the mind and tries the faith.

### . . . A surprising discovery

Having spent a considerable part of my life ministering to those who suffer and to those who care for them I have been made aware of a surprising fact. Those who suffer rarely complain about their suffering being a barrier to belief in God. It is almost always those who have to watch their relatives or friends suffer who encounter the most difficulty. Often, in the face of suffering, the latter project their sense of helplessness onto God. Some become bitter in their criticism of God's apparent incompetence. Disparagingly he is portrayed as a divine 'touch judge' who periodically makes a fuss on the fringe of the action but has no real authority to influence the game. In contrast a few others vent their feelings of anger against a God who, far from standing helplessly on the sidelines, is entirely responsible for the action in the form of the senseless suffering being endured before their very eyes. Many others nurse a deep-seated hurt or a bewildered disappointment that their prayers for healing have not been answered.

Yet, frequently and surprisingly, those who suffer most reveal few of these marks of bitterness, resentment or anger. And, if they do, they rarely harden into a permanent attitude of mind. Indeed, some of the strongest testimonies to faith in God and some of the most beautiful demonstrations of love, selflessness and service come from those who endure the greatest pain. This particular truth is strikingly illustrated in some words of Jean Vanier, who writes in his book *The Broken Body*:

> If you enter into relationship
> with a lonely or suffering person
> you will discover something else:
> that it is you who are being healed.
> The broken person will reveal to you
> your own hurt and the hardness of your heart,
> but *also* how much *you* are loved.
> Thus the one you came to heal
> becomes your healer.

Nevertheless, although 'good' can often emerge out of suffering, it is difficult to justify suffering and virtually impossible to 'glorify' it. Suffering forever remains a reality which defies intellectual justification. Even Jesus didn't try to explain it.Nor, for that matter, did God when faced with the suffering of Job.

## THE PATIENCE OF JOB . . .

Sooner or later anyone writing a chapter on suffering would be expected to arrive at the book of Job and to the famous story of that virtuous and right-living man, who had to endure undeserved suffering with commendable patience. The patience of Job is legendary. In actual fact, though Job had many virtues, patience was not one of them. Indeed, on careful reading, the story reveals his impatience with people who insisted on telling him exactly why he was suffering.

I think I know the feeling. Some years ago, following a major heart attack, I was told, by one friend after another, precisely why it had happened. Such was the intensity of their desire to get the message across to me that I began to feel quite guilty for daring to have a heart attack in the first place. One of the few people who didn't pontificate was my cardiologist. He had more sense. He told me how it happened. He didn't presume to tell me why. He said, that he didn't know.

Job's 'friends' were not so reticent – and he wasn't best pleased. He was an awkward sort of customer who didn't take kindly to smooth-talkers pronouncing premature judgement on his afflictions. Losing his home, his family and his health was bad enough without having to cope with visitors equipped with the so-called conventional wisdom of the day, namely, that suffering was the direct result of his personal wickedness. Who needs enemies when you have friends like that?

But if Job revealed little patience regarding his friends,

he wasn't all that patient towards God either. In fact he was downright argumentative! Like the writer of Psalm 73, 'there's no justice' could well have summed up his feelings. Job knew that the assessment of his friends was wrong. Their grand theories didn't match up with the reality of his experience. Indeed, as God later revealed, not only had they found the wrong answers; they had been asking the wrong questions. Job took the matter up with God in no uncertain terms, correctly assuming that God welcomed free speech. God's answer when it came, though forming one of the most sublime pieces of literature of all time (Job 38–42), gave no explanation of his suffering. Job didn't seem to mind. It was enough that God had spoken. He was not forsaken. God put the record straight by recognising his innocence and refusing to endorse the accusations of his friends. God was just. And Job was relieved, for justice had been the real problem – not suffering. Suffering remained a mystery.

**THE MYSTERY OF SUFFERING . . .**

If we are even to begin to penetrate the mystery we must turn from Job to Jesus. From the man whose undeserved suffering mercifully came to an end in restored health and fortune, to the one who drank the cup of suffering down to, and including, the very dregs. Some of the graphic details of that suffering are to be found in St Mark's story of the crucifixion.

The passers-by jeered at him; they shook their heads and said, 'Aha! So you would destroy the Temple and rebuild it in three days! Then save yourself; come down from the cross!' The chief priests and the scribes mocked him among themselves in the same way with the words,

'He saved others, he cannot save himself. Let the Christ, the king of Israel, come down from the cross now, for us to see it and believe.' Even those who were crucified with him taunted him. When the sixth hour came there was darkness over the whole land until the ninth hour. And at the ninth hour Jesus cried out with a loud voice . . . *'My God, my God, why have you forsaken me?'*

Mark 15:29–34

*. . . Why me? Why you?*

Nowhere else is the agony of personal suffering so exposed as in those words of Jesus, 'My God, my God, why have you forsaken me?' On the surface the words give expression not only to intense physical suffering but also, it would seem, to deep mental torture. The physical pain was bad enough but the intellectual and moral questions posed by the pain are even worse. Suffering always produces questions and in this cry of Jesus from the cross there were several basic ones.

Why me? On the lips of Jesus that question had a particular poignancy. He was known as the healer. The one who eased the suffering of others, who cured sickness and removed pain wherever he encountered it. Now he is engulfed and seemingly overwhelmed by it. Suffering not only the physical pain but also the cruel taunt, 'He saved others, he cannot save himself.'

But there was another 'why' in the suffering of Jesus which only served to intensify it. That was the 'Why you?' with reference to God his Father. He could understand Judas' betrayal, Peter's denial, the disciples falling asleep in Gethsemane and all but a few absent from the cross, but 'Why had God above all others abandoned him?' At the beginning of his earthly work, when he was baptised in the River Jordan, his Father had not remained silent,

109

quite the reverse. There had been strong affirmation, 'You are my Son, the Beloved; my favour rests on you' (Mark 1:11).

In the light of such words we can well understand the pain of disappointment and desertion contained in the question, 'Why God . . . why you?'

*. . . A man alone*

The personal heart attack, to which I referred earlier in this chapter, happened while I was in London so I ended up staying in Westminster Hospital for a period of three weeks. For the first five days, with the co-operation of the nursing staff, I remained incognito and as my condition improved, I began to enjoy the freedom of not being known as a bishop. On the sixth day the Archbishop of Canterbury visited me – and my cover was blown. That evening, and every other evening during the remainder of my stay in hospital, there was a queue of patients at my bedside wanting to share their problems with me. In almost every case they came to see me after their visitors had gone or if they had not had any visitors. It was then that they were at their most vulnerable. It was then that their 'aloneness' caught up with them.

I had exactly the same feelings, and so, apparently, did Jesus. The depth of his suffering was contained in that word 'forsaken'. The three hours of darkness that surrounded him before he uttered his anguished cry symbolised the aloneness that he felt. Rejection by others was not new to him. He had been alienated by his family and community. Even his own inner circle of friends, his disciples, had melted away. But this was something different. Forsaken and abandoned by God. Darkness replacing light. God remaining silent and hidden.

### . . . *A way forward*

Some years ago a most refreshing translation of the New Testament was produced by J. B. Phillips. Mr Phillips had a remarkable capacity for making the Scriptures come alive with his skilful and imaginative use of language. What many people don't know is that he suffered from severe depression. His widow, speaking of his depression wrote, 'Jack found himself sharing the darkness with his friend Michael Hollings, and in the dark experience of his pain he could only repeat Michael's words, "There is no way out, only a way forward." '

It was not dissimilar for Jesus, nor is it very different for many others who walk through the valley of suffering and pain. In the Garden of Gethsemane Jesus, it seemed, longed for a way out: 'Abba, Father!' he said. 'For you everything is possible. Take this cup away from me.' But he also recognised that there was only a way forward when he went on to say, 'But let it be as you, not I, would have it.' It was that willingness to go forward that took him to the cross to endure the suffering not for his own sins but for the sins of the world. Having put his hand to that particular plough there was no going back, only forward – to finish the task, even though it meant dereliction. In taking upon himself the burden of the world's sin, he was committing himself to suffering the ultimate consequence of that sin, namely, separation from God.

The mystery contained in these remarkable words of Jesus, and the depth of the suffering which they convey, is unfathomable. In trying to understand them we can only, as it were, catch glimpses of light at the edges of the curtain of darkness. However, of one thing we can be sure, in the midst of his suffering Jesus lost the sense of his Father's presence. He felt forsaken and abandoned by God. A man alone, suffering – and enduring the emptiness of affliction. Though we shall never know, some words of Simone Weil may come close to the truth:

> Affliction constrained Christ to implore that he might be spared; to seek consolation from man; to believe that he was forsaken by the Father. It forced a just man to cry out against God . . . This is no blasphemy but a genuine cry of anguish . . . Affliction makes God appear to be absent for a time, more absent than a dead man, more absent than light in the utter darkness of a cell. A kind of horror submerges the whole soul . . . The soul has to go on loving in the emptiness, or at least to go on wanting to love . . .

A GOD WHO SUFFERS . . .

It is significant that in our consideration of the 'problem', or mystery, of suffering we have arrived at the cross of Christ. For there, in what Christians believe to be the pivotal point of history, God is revealed as one who suffers. A God who, despite all appearances to the contrary, refuses to stand aloof from the suffering of his children. There are glimpses of this truth, of course, throughout the ministry of Jesus as he identified with the sick and sorrowful. We are given a particular insight in Matthew 25 where Jesus teaches that suffering inflicted upon his brothers is really affliction directed at him, 'In so far as you did this to one of the least of these brothers of mine, you did it to me.' In other words he suffers with all those who suffer.

Supremely, however, we see this truth portrayed at Calvary. God presents himself to the world in a whole variety of ways, including creation, but uniquely he reveals himself in the person of Jesus Christ. 'He who has seen me,' said Jesus, 'has seen the Father'. Central to the portrayal by Jesus of the loving Father was his suffering and death. 'God so loved the world that he gave his only Son . . .' Indeed when Paul wrote to the young church at Corinth (2 Corinthians 5) he made this amazing statement about God's involvement at the cross: 'God was in Christ reconciling the world to himself.' God was no mere spectator of the crucifixion. He was totally involved in the suffering it entailed.

### . . . No absentee

A simple little story attributed to a young unnamed cancer patient helps to make the point: he dreamt that he was walking along the beach with his Lord. Across the sky flashed scenes from his life. For each scene he noticed two sets of footprints in the sand, one belonging to him, the other to the Lord. When the last scene of his life flashed before him he looked back at the footprints on the sand. He noticed that many times along the path of his life there was only one set of footprints. He also noticed that it happened at the very lowest and saddest times of his life. This really bothered him, and he questioned the Lord about it. 'Lord, you said that, once I decided to follow you, you would walk with me all the way – but I've noticed that during the most difficult times in my life there was only one set of footprints. I don't understand why, in times when I needed you most, you would leave me.' The Lord replied, 'My precious child, I love you and would never leave you during your trials and sufferings. When you see only one set of footprints, it was then I carried you.'

Here is the paradox: Jesus felt forsaken – that was the most bitter of his sufferings. Yet, God was not absent. He

113

was there in the emptiness, darkness and despair. Hidden, silent – but there, deeply and crucially identified with suffering. And the evidence for that, strangely enough, is the cross itself. You see, the only visible body which God presented to the world was that of his Son who suffers pain and death on a cross. God there declares his solidarity with all his suffering children. Indeed, it might be said, that only such a God dare stand before a suffering and broken world.

Listen to some rather stark, almost shocking, words from the German pastor and theologian Dietrich Bonhoeffer, which he wrote from prison, shortly before his execution at the hands of the Nazis:

> God let himself be pushed out of the world on to the Cross. He is weak and powerless in the world, and that is precisely the way, the only way, in which he is with us and helps us. Matthew 8:17 makes it quite clear that Christ helps us, not by virtue of his omnipotence, but by virtue of weakness and suffering . . . Only the Suffering God can help. That is a reversal of what the religious man expects from God. Man is summoned to share in God's suffering at the hands of a godless world.

The uniqueness of Christianity lies in this fact perhaps more than any other, namely, that Christians worship and follow a God who suffers, not only in theory but in practice.

### . . . No hands but our hands

Those who have to watch their loved ones suffer are understandably more concerned with practice than theory. It is one thing to be aware intellectually that God suffers with us, but quite another to be assured that he will do something about it. It is intervention for which people long and pray. God understands such feelings which is why every day he brings practical comfort, help and healing to those who suffer. For just as Jesus was the visible and tangible expression of God's love and care for the suffering of his day, so are we in our day.

God has no hands but our hands and he comes to those who suffer in and through the selfless love and healing touch of his other children. He comes to them in well-known people like Mother Teresa, Sheila Cassidy, Cicely Saunders and a host of others. And he comes in a multitude of unknown and unsung people who are to be found in every community across the land and across the world. Many of them would make no claim to Christian faith but they share a common concern to help those in need. In homes, hospices and hospitals, day in and day out, God comes in healing through the ministry of all those who care for the sick and dying. It is my sincere belief that all healing comes from God and that God comes in all healing. It was my predecessor as Bishop of Bradford, Donald Coggan, who wrote, 'Wherever the forces of darkness, disease and evil are driven back, there the Kingdom of God comes and God enters more fully into the sovereignty of his own world.'

Christians are specifically called to walk in the footsteps of Jesus. If we do so he will lead us to the poor, weak, lonely, oppressed and suffering. And he will lead us to them not with theories nor with preconceived solutions, but with peace, love and hope. He will also reveal, as he did in Matthew 25, that not only does he suffer with those who suffer, but that he is hidden in the weak and suffering – awaiting our love, compassion and care.

When God answered Job he didn't explain the suffering but he put it and Job into perspective. Jesus through his cross and resurrection does the same thing. His disciples repudiated the cross. They tried to dissuade him from it. They could only see it in terms of defeat and death, evil and ignominy. And, of course, it was all these things until it was placed within the context of the resurrection. Then it took on new meaning and significance.

In the hands of Jesus suffering and death were transformed. Suffering became creative rather than destructive, redeeming rather than degrading. It became the means whereby he could identify fully with suffering humanity and the means of their ultimate deliverance from fear of every kind.

Appearances can be so deceptive. On that first Good Friday evil appeared rampant and triumphant, while goodness appeared vanquished. To all intents and purposes Calvary could only be described in destructive terms. In reality, as the first Easter Day clearly declared, it was transformed into the most creative and redeeming act of all time. It was Jurgen Moltman, the German theologian, who put it like this:

> Through his own abandonment by God, the crucified Christ brings God to those who are abandoned by God. Through his sufferings he brings salvation to those who suffer. Through his death he brings eternal life to those who are dying.

What looked like defeat was turned into victory. Such was the transformation. Suffering like death was not a useless cul de sac. There may not always be a way out but, thanks be to Jesus, there is a creative way forward in the purpose and love of God.

## Questions

1. Do you think it is right to be angry when faced with suffering which is obviously undeserved?
2. What would you say to someone who is bitter because God seems to be 'taking it out' on innocent people while ignoring those who are behaving selfishly or cruelly towards others?
3. Have you ever analysed your own thoughts during a serious illness? What were your feelings towards God? Was your faith diminished or enriched as a result of the experience of suffering?
4. 'No way out, only a way forward.' If asked to do so, how would you explain the way forward, in a creative and sensitive manner, to a friend who had a terminal illness?
5. 'A God who suffers may have something to say to the poor and disadvantaged of the world but has he anything relevant to say to a society which places increasing emphasis on self-reliance?' How would you answer that question?

# 9

# There Is Nothing that Is Not Holy
*God in the totality of life*

Life is full of surprises, including the life of a bishop. Frequently I am asked what surprised me most when I became a bishop. Without hesitation, I am able to respond, 'The sheer volume of correspondence that lands daily on my desk.' I simply wouldn't have believed that it could be so incessant and so varied. Much of it is routine. Some of it is important. A lot of it is encouraging. And a little of it is cranky – to put it mildly!

One particular type of letter has been arriving with monotonous regularity in recent years. Its contents usually begin with a question and end with a statement. Sometimes they are couched in courteous tones, quite often they are expressed in belligerent terms. The question is, 'Why doesn't the Church keep out of politics?' and the statement is, 'Religion and politics don't mix.'

Now I have no particular axe to grind on this matter and sometimes the criticisms levelled at the pronouncements of some Church leaders are entirely justified. The Church is not above criticism and should need no protection from it. Nevertheless there is something fundamentally wrong in the content of both the question and the statement. Indeed, they carry unfortunate and unfair implications for the many religious and Christian men and women who so effectively engage in the political life of our country.

## WATERTIGHT COMPARTMENTS? . . .

The suggestion that the Church should keep out of politics and that religion and politics don't mix reveals a very interesting and not uncommon view of life. A somewhat similar view is held by those who claim that, 'Religion is a private and personal affair that has nothing whatsoever to do with our public life.' The clear implication of such sincerely held views is that life is a series of separate compartments, one of which is marked 'religion'. This particular compartment appears to be watertight to prevent spillage over into other compartments of life and, I presume, to prevent pollution seeping in to religion from contaminating contact with the outside world.

### . . . Sacred and secular

Before my readers begin to protest that I am stretching a point let me say at once that I witness a similar division of life into sacred and secular categories every day. I can even see such a division within myself. Words spoken to a Rotary Club on Friday about priorities for a pluralist society are called 'a talk'. Almost the same words, spoken in church on Sunday, are given the grand title of 'sermon'. The former is seen as secular, the latter as sacred. Reading the Bible is considered by some to be sacred, while reading a novel is without doubt a secular pastime. Going to church falls within the sacred category, while going to watch a football match is very much in the secular mould. If you wear a clerical dog-collar you are very definitely in the sacred ministry, whereas if you serve (which is another name for ministry) the needs of a community, as a member of another profession, you are following a secular calling. To care for the poor is a spiritual and sacred occupation.

To ask about the cause of poverty is political dynamite and a secular concern.

Now, of course, there are distinctions within life which need to be categorised for the sake of convenience. That's why so many of our newspapers are getting so large that they won't come through our letter-boxes. They are subdivided into special sections which are directed at most of the major aspects and interests of life. Our growth towards greater maturity in life is governed to a large extent by the balanced development of the physical, intellectual, spiritual and social aspects of our lives. Sporting, family, business and cultural interests all make distinctive contributions to the wholeness of life. That wholeness can be jeopardised if we insist on keeping the different aspects of our lives in separate, watertight compartments. Yet many people do, and a considerable number of them see the sacred and the secular as poles apart and some of them, with a sense of guilt, spend their time swinging backwards and forwards between the two.

I well remember my own sense of guilt when as a young curate my vicar came to visit me unexpectedly and discovered me reading a detective novel. I found myself making all sorts of excuses as to why that particular type of literature was in my hand rather than something more 'holy' or more edifying! Even today I'm still aware of a similar embarrassment on the part of some of my acquaintances when they invite me to their home for a meal. A few minutes before the meal begins I am usually conscious of mental gymnastics taking place and a whispered conversation being held, which goes something like this, 'Since the Bishop is here shouldn't we ask him to say grace? Will he be offended if we don't?' And so I am prevailed upon to 'do the necessary' – much to my embarrassment, for it casts me in the sacred mould; and much to the surprise of some of the other guests, who are inadvertently classified as the secular lot – for they never say grace before meals at other times. For a few minutes the ensuing conversation is usually rather stilted for when a bishop has just been overheard talking to God how do you change the subject without being rude? Fortunately by the time the main course arrives the conversation has returned to normal.

A FALSE DIVISION . . .

It's funny but Jesus also had problems when eating out. People had certain expectations of him which he refused to fulfil. It wasn't so much the things he said as the company he kept. All was well as long as he mixed with religious people and did religious things. It was when he dined out in the company of outcasts and sinners – the secular lot – that he came in for such sharp criticism. Like, for instance, in Luke 7:36–50, when he found himself at the same table as a somewhat notorious woman, and treated her with respect and received her worship. The religious leaders of his day were scandalised by such conduct on this and other occasions and complained bitterly, 'This man welcomes sinners and eats with them' (Luke 15:2). Jesus wasn't put off by such a negative attitude. In fact he used such carping criticism as an opportunity for some positive teaching about God in his famous story of the Prodigal Son. God's concerns, far from being narrowly religious, encompass every aspect of life.

. . . Not just religion but life

It is a great mistake to think that God is only interested in religion. That is an extremely naive and limited view that cannot be sustained from the Bible – especially from

121

some of the prophets, like Amos, Micah and Haggai, who spoke so forcefully on behalf of God. Through their words to their particular generation God revealed that his concerns were social rather than religious. Prophets like Amos simply wouldn't have understood the statement that religion and politics don't mix. He and others took it upon themselves to engage in politics and they had some very pertinent and wise things to say about relationships between Israel and the other nations of the world. As Lord Blanch, former Archbishop of York, wrote, 'They looked askance at the social life of their people and the commercial and economic structures of their day, in which the rich became richer and the poor became poorer (Amos 6), in which profit was the only standard of success (Amos 8:5), and in which inflation was rampant (Haggai 1:6).' In their view a holy God was not interested only in how people behaved on the Sabbath but in how they lived their lives the rest of the week. The whole of the Bible is a story about a God who is concerned with everything that is in the world – both sacred and secular.

Jesus certainly held similar views. Like his Father he was concerned with the totality of life. He was exasperated with, and reserved some of his strongest words for, those who criticised him for doing 'good works' on the Sabbath. Such people were appalled that he would be so insensitive as to heal people on a day that was set aside for religious purposes only. He was astounded that people could be so narrowly religious as to refuse acts of mercy and compassion to those in need, whatever the day. Their criticism provoked from him the well-known words, 'The Sabbath is made for man and not man for the Sabbath.' Our Lord was not setting aside the Sabbath (or Sunday as it became for the Christian) as of no importance, quite the reverse. He wanted people to see it in positive terms as a day of rest and recreation rather than misery and restriction. One day of rest in seven is a divine provision for the health and wholeness of humankind, and people and nations ignore it at their peril. But God, in calling the Sabbath 'holy', was not implying that other days were not. On the contrary, the Sabbath is not just a religious observance, whether it be for Jews on Saturday or Christians on Sunday. It is an attitude to life. It is a weekly reminder that the whole of life is sacred and not just certain parts of it.


## THERE IS NOTHING THAT IS NOT HOLY . . .

It was Paul Tillich, the German theologian, who wrote these now famous words which form the title of this chapter. While not everyone would wish to agree with him, his words appear to me to be a very pertinent comment on the totality of life. They also serve as a very powerful reminder of the danger of making too sharp a distinction between the sacred and the secular. Of course such a distinction tends to make life easier for us. It is always more comfortable when we have stereotyped people and things and placed them in their appropriate pigeon-holes. Life becomes tidier and more predictable when we know exactly where the boundaries are in our relationships with things and people – and God.

The trouble is that God insists on surprising us by making nonsense of our convenient categories. He confuses us by refusing to accept our simplistic stereotyping. Instead he comes to us from the most unexpected places and speaks to us from the most unlikely people – including those with little or no religious affiliation or conviction. Listen to the words of Brian Keenan soon after his release from being held hostage in Beirut for nearly four years. Asked if religion had helped him during his captivity, he replied, 'I am not and never was religious in terms of an institutionalised church. But in the days when I was kept locked up alone, I found that one cannot keep the mind alive by talking just to itself. If you are asking me did I pray, the answer is yes. If you are asking me am I religious then no.'

### . . . As God sees it

It was Michel Quoist, the author of the well-known *Prayers of Life* who wrote, 'If only we knew how to look at life as God sees it, we would realise that nothing is secular in the world, but that everything contributes to the building of the kingdom of God.' I think this is what the writer of the book of Ecclesiasticus had in mind when he wrote his famous passage (38:34) in which he affirms those engaged in the pursuit of their so-called secular calling in commerce and industry. 'They sustain the structure of the world, and their prayer is concerned with their trade.' In other words, their work is their prayer and there is no dividing line between them. George Herbert expressed the same truth in his famous hymn:

> Teach me, my God and King,
> in all things thee to see;
> and what I do in anything
> to do it as for thee.
>
> A servant with this clause
> makes drudgery divine;
> who sweeps a room, as for thy laws,
> makes that and the action fine.
>
> This is the famous stone
> that turneth all to gold;

for that which God doth touch and own
cannot for less be told.

Some of the finest Christians of modern time have been
those who have given notable public service within the
secular structures of the nation. People like Len Murray
whose wise and courageous leadership of the T.U.C.
earned admiration, nation-wide respect and the gratitude
of the Queen in the award of a life peerage in 1985. Yet
undergirding all his so-called secular activity was a deep
faith in God and a strong conviction that in serving the
practical needs of his fellow trade-unionists he was pro-
moting the Kingdom of God. The same is true of Lord
Tonypandy, one of the most cheerful and friendly members of the House of Lords. As George Thomas he was an
ebullient Member of Parliament, a brilliant Speaker of the
House of Commons – and a fiery lay-preacher from the
Welsh valleys. He saw no conflict between his full involvement in the cut and thrust of social and political life and
his sincerely held and wonderfully infectious Christian
faith. Like the God whom they worshipped and served
they, and countless others like them, saw life in whole
terms. The essence of pure religion for them, as for James
in his epistle (1:27), consisted in the practical application
of the love of God to the needs of society. They were
determined to seek and serve God wherever God was to
be found in human life.


GOD'S WORLD – AND OUR HOME . . .

We should not be surprised that God can be found in
every aspect of human experience in the life of the world.
After all, the world is his and he made it. The magnificent
and beautiful story with which the Bible begins depicts

125

God in action in the creation of the universe. That story provides us with a very powerful introduction to many of the contemporary problems and challenges that confront the human race. It also introduces us to one of the main themes of the Christian faith, namely that the world and everything in it depends upon God for its existence.

Of course, some will wish to debate both the method and the detail of creation and that is entirely proper. But, at the end of the day, the clear teaching of the Bible and the universal tradition of the Church affirm belief in God as the Creator of all. The Jewish and Christian Scriptures begin with the statement that 'in the beginning God created heaven and earth.' Likewise the Christian creeds begin by corporately expressing faith in the Creator God, 'We believe in one God, the Father, the Almighty, Maker of heaven and earth.'

But God's creation of the world is matched by his love for the world. What is arguably the best known verse in the Bible, John 3:16, begins, 'God so loved the world . . .'. It is just worth noting that it doesn't begin, 'God so loved the Church', though something rather similar is found elsewhere. It doesn't even say, 'God so loved people', though that is taken for granted. It says, and the word is *cosmos*, that 'God so loved the *world*', that is the whole created order and system, 'that he gave his only Son'. For the Church? Yes. For all people? Yes. But for the material order and for the environment, surely not? But the answer is again a resounding yes. It is we who have limited the words and twisted the meaning to mean us – and the rest can look after itself. Perhaps that's why we so readily divide the sacred from the secular and why we so quickly assume that God is only interested in the spiritual and not in the material. But it won't do. God loves the world, despite its corruptions and shortcomings, because it is his.

The measure of his love for it is the gift of his only Son for its salvation.

A few months ago, one of the colour supplements of the Sunday papers had some quite remarkable photographs taken from outer space. One of them was accompanied by these words from an American astronaut:

> Suddenly there emerges a sparkling
> blue and white jewel,
> a light, delicate sky-blue sphere
> laced with slowly swirling veils of white.
> It takes more than a moment to realise
> this is earth . . . *home*!

'God saw all that he had made, and indeed it was very good.' We live in a wonderful planet, in a beautiful world. We are solemnly charged by God with the task of looking after it, for it is not only his world – it is our home.

## THE GREEN GOSPEL . . .

The lessons we learn best in life are nearly always those we are forced to learn the hard way. The lesson regarding my responsibility for the care of the world which is my home I learnt as a result of a moment of great embarrassment. I was driving through the Lincolnshire town of Grantham at the time and was caught in a long line of cars at some traffic lights. Having both hands free for a moment I took the opportunity to pop a piece of chocolate in my mouth and throw the wrapping paper out of the window. I was just about to close the window when a policeman appeared – holding my wrapping paper in his hand. 'Sir,' he said, 'we are trying to keep our town as clean as possible. Please, will you take your rubbish with you when you leave?' If only the ground could have opened and swallowed me up!

But, since divine intervention of that kind seemed out of the question, I muttered an embarrassed apology, took the wrapping paper, let in the clutch and, at a discreet speed of course, left the scene of the crime. As I drove away I was full of anger. To be honest I was angry at being caught and embarrassed. But on reflection I ended up being full of admiration for the courtesy and concern of the unknown constable who had taught me a lesson I have never forgotten. We are all responsible for the care of our environment. If we misuse or exploit it, through indifference or self-interest, it is our grandchildren who will suffer – and they won't thank us for it.

### . . . *A universal challenge*

Of course it's not just a matter of keeping the streets tidy – though that is important. The crucial nature of the problem may best be illustrated by the words of a modern continental theologian who has made a special study and written extensively on the issue:

> What we call the environmental crisis is not merely a crisis in the natural environment of human beings. It is nothing less than a crisis in human beings themselves. It is a crisis of life on this planet, a crisis so comprehensive and so irreversible that it cannot be unjustly described as apocalyptic. It is not a temporary crisis. As far as we can judge, it is the beginning of a life and death struggle for creation on this earth.

These are strong words but they certainly help to put the matter into perspective. God's concern for creation and the material order is beyond question. Therefore, we must accept our responsibility to share that concern and give practical expression to it.

## . . . And job description

But what is the content of that responsibility? Have we a 'job description' that we can follow? I have heard the task described in a number of ways, two of which I find particularly helpful. We are charged by God to be *stewards* – to manage carefully and wisely the earth's resources entrusted to us. We are *custodians* – required not just to manage but to enhance our inheritance with the future in mind. But perhaps the concept of *partnership* is the one which most accurately describes our relationship to creation and the care of the environment. When Paul wrote his letter to the Roman Christians he included a rather complex, but extremely important, passage (Romans 8:19–25) with reference to creation. The words seem to imply that the gospel, or good news, of God was not only that men and women were to be set free by the death and resurrection of Jesus, but so also was creation. Paul declares that it is God's intention '. . . that the whole of creation itself might be freed from its slavery to corruption and brought into the same glorious freedom as the children of God.'

As stewards and custodians we are to share with God in that care of creation which reflects his love for it and his refusal to abandon it. Indeed we are to play our full part in helping to realise God's purpose for creation. A purpose, the fulfilment of which, says Paul, is the very thing for which creation itself longs, 'We are well aware that the whole creation . . . has been groaning in labour pains. . . . waiting . . . to be set free.'

*. . . Yes – that means us!*

Now we all have our own horror stories to tell about pollution, acid rain, the ozone layer, global warming and the tons of litter removed daily from our streets. We can very quickly reach the stage when we become paralysed by the sheer magnitude of the problem – so we back off and leave it to 'the others' to do something about it. Of course it isn't always easy to get the balance of concern right. The issues are not always as clear-cut as some would have us believe. But all of us have some small corner in which we can demonstrate our care for the environment. There are practical things that we each can do – like the use of unleaded petrol and ozone-friendly aerosols. We might even keep our chocolate wrappings in the car rather than toss them out the window!

I am told that Sir Matt Busby, the former manager of Manchester United, gave a simple piece of advice to his players which helped to produce the quality football played by his famous 'Busby Babes':

> Do the simple thing
> Do it well and
> Do it now.

That is also a sound piece of advice in exercising our proper care of the environment. We must not see it in material terms as opposed to the spiritual. We must not see our personal relationship to God as sacred and our relationship to creation as secular. There is nothing that is not holy. God loves and cares for the material world as well as the people in it. We live in a beautiful world. It makes sense to look after it.

When a bishop is installed in his cathedral church at the beginning of his ministry the service ends with a simple

yet significant piece of ritual. As the highly coloured ceremony draws to a close the bishop moves to the great West
door which, as he approaches it, is thrown open for him
to move out into the world. It is a powerful symbol that
our discovery of God and our worship of God do not
take place primarily in church but outside in the open
world . . . for there is nothing that is not holy.


## Questions

1. Do you think that religion is a personal and private
   affair? How would you convince someone that it was
   not?
2. A friend of mine is a doctor. He is also a Christian
   minister. During the week he heals the sick. On Sunday
   he preaches the gospel. Would you place his weekday
   and weekend activities in different categories?
3. 'A servant with this clause makes drudgery divine': are
   such sentiments totally unrealistic in today's world?
4. Can a proper concern for the environment be described
   as a Christian concern? Do you think that the description of the environmental crisis as a 'life and death
   struggle' is going too far?
5. Steward – Custodian – Partner: which of these three
   models do you think is the most accurate?

# 10

# Something Better than Optimism
*Christian hope in a world of uncertainty*

Not long ago I came across a lovely and humorous little story about twin boys who, although they looked like 'peas in a pod' were, in nature and temperament, as different as chalk and cheese. One was excessively pessimistic while the other was extremely optimistic. For one, every cloud had a silver lining; for the other, every silver lining had a dirty great cloud in the middle!

Their parents felt they ought to encourage each of them to have a slightly more balanced and realistic view of life. So for the twins' tenth birthday they thought up a scheme which they were convinced would help to change the extreme attitude of each of the boys. They bought their pessimistic son a super bicycle, the latest and most popular model – surely this would cheer him up. At the same time they filled a plastic bag full of manure for their optimistic son – surely that would dampen his enthusiasm. It's difficult to get enthusiastic about manure unless you are a keen gardener! They hid the presents in different parts of the house but, unfortunately, the boys discovered the hiding places the night before their birthday and were able to have a sneak preview.

That night as the boys climbed into bed the optimist asked his brother, 'What have they got you?' 'Oh, it's a disaster,' he replied. 'They've got me a bike and I'm sure to break my neck riding it', he groaned. 'By the way,' he

said, 'what have they got you?' His brother smiled brightly
and, with a heart obviously throbbing with excitement,
whispered hoarsely, 'I think they've got me a pony!'

## SOMETHING BETTER THAN OPTIMISM . . .

In introducing the theme of hope I use the above story
not in order to despise pessimism nor to glorify optimism.
There is nothing wrong with being pessimistic or optimistic if that is the way God has made us. Some of us are
born pessimists and some are born optimists. Most of us
are somewhere in the middle though on occasions we
swing towards one extreme or the other. But from the
outset I want to stress that hope is not purely a matter of
temperament. Pessimism without hope can lead to
despair. Optimism without hope can result in starry-eyed
fantasy totally devoid of reality. Hope is more than optimism.

### . . . And more than wishful thinking

Day in and day out I hear people give expression to their
hope in a form of words which, when examined closely,
carries very little conviction and hardly any genuine expectation. 'I hope it won't rain', some say, even though the
clouds are dark and low, and they themselves are carrying
an umbrella. 'I'm hoping for the best', say others, even
though, because of lack of effort and foresight, they certainly don't deserve it. 'Everything will turn out right in
the end', we say, even when we have made foolish mistakes and completely frustrated our own carefully laid
plans. 'I hope something will turn up', we declare, though
we have no idea what, or why it should do so. Often
there is no real possibility that what we are hoping for

will actually come to pass, and we justify such an attitude by saying, 'There's no harm in hoping.' But, in truth, it is little more than wishful thinking.

One of the classic stories told by Jesus was about a man whose hope had all the characteristics of wishful thinking – with disastrous results. He was a builder by trade and in order to get his house up quickly he decided to cut a few corners – like dispensing with a proper survey and a well-laid foundation. But he achieved his objective. The house was completed and, perhaps, at the 'topping out' ceremony the hope was expressed that it would stand for ever. Some hope – for a house built on sand! It was simply wishful thinking, for we read the words of Jesus: 'But everyone who listens to these words of mine and does not act on them will be like a stupid man who built his house on sand. Rain came down, floods rose, gales blew and struck that house, and it fell; and what a fall it had!' (Matthew 7:26–7) Hope is obviously more than wishful thinking.


*. . . And more than self-confidence*

The hope which many other people have is based not so much on wishful thinking as on supreme self-confidence, allied to past experience and achievement. 'We've managed to cope with everything life has thrown at us thus far, so we expect to be able to cope with anything the future may hold', is the philosophy which inspires such hope. In other words, to use a popular expression from the world of the theatre: 'It will be all right on the night.'

The saying, of course, is associated with a rather chaotic dress rehearsal in which everything seems to go wrong and, with the opening night only hours away, despair threatens. At that point, on the basis of past experience, come the words of reassurance: 'It will be all right on the night.'

But it needs to be said, also on the basis of past experience, that such hope is not always justified. Recently, during an interview on Radio Two, I heard a well-known actor describing his own particular nightmare in this regard. He and a fellow actor at one point in a rather serious play had to carry a corpse off the stage on a stretcher. It was such a simple thing to do that other more important matters crowded it out of the rehearsals – with somewhat disastrous and hilarious results on the opening night. At the crucial moment in the play when they picked up the stretcher they discovered that, unfortunately, they had positioned themselves back to back and were beginning to walk away from each other – much to the disadvantage of the corpse. With massive dignity and great aplomb they put the stretcher down, adjusted their positions, and picked the stretcher up again to find that they were now facing each other and, like the corpse, were unable to move. It became all right on the night – at the third attempt. Next day they took no chances and rehearsed the scene for an hour.

There's all the difference in the world between genuine hope and mere wishful thinking, between misplaced self-confidence and well-founded expectation. Real hope persists despite discouragements. It is better than optimism. It perseveres against all the odds.

IT SPRINGS ETERNAL . . .

It is about the kind of hope that Alexander Pope wrote in his *Essay on Man*:

> Hope springs eternal in the human breast,
> Man never is, but always to be blest.

Pope quite obviously touched on a remarkable and vital aspect of human life. Hope, it seems, is an essential component of the human spirit even in the most unlikely circumstances. Charles Dickens, in one of his famous and classic novels *Nicholas Nickleby*, seemed to speak for the human spirit when he said, 'Hope to the last . . . always hope; . . . Never leave off hoping; it doesn't answer . . . Don't leave a stone unturned. It's always something to know you've done the best you could. But don't leave off hoping, or it's no use doing anything. Hope, hope, to the last.'

We see clear evidence of the tenacity of hope throughout history and right into the present day. Marie Curie and Florence Nightingale are but two examples. But, within living memory of most of us, perhaps Martin Luther King is one of the outstanding examples. Humanly speaking he ought to have had all the hope crushed out of him in his encounter with the rampant racism of the southern States of America in the 1950s and '60s. Maligned and misunderstood, persecuted and eventually assassinated, his human spirit refused to relinquish its hold on hope. The unconquerable nature of that hope was revealed to the world in his now famous 'I have a dream' speech in which the content of his hope was spelt out in words like:

I have a dream that one day the state of Alabama . . . will be transformed into a situation where little black boys and black girls will be able to join hands with little white boys and white girls and walk together as sisters and brothers . . . that day when all of God's children, black men and white men, Jews and Gentiles, Protestants and Catholics, will be able to join hands and sing in the words of the old Negro spiritual, 'Free at last! Free at last! Thank God Almighty, we are free at last!'

But perhaps some less well-known words of his provide the real key to understanding the nature of the hope which sprang eternal in his heart. They are truly remarkable in the depth of their insight: 'Good defeated is stronger than evil triumphant.' It is that kind of human hope which has burned in the hearts of men and women since time began. In Yorkshire we have seen a local example of this in recent days. John Hawkridge, a Bradford lad, was born with a serious physical handicap. Despite the efforts of the medical profession it seemed that walking unaided for only a few yards was the limit of his expectations. Certainly any thought of trekking across the famous Yorkshire Moors was a dream beyond imagining. But hope really does spring eternal in the human breast and a recent television documentary filmed John walking and climbing in the Himalayas and reaching a height of fifteen thousand feet up Mount Everest.

One can only admire those who refuse to lie down under adverse circumstances or who are determined not to be defeated by anything which life may throw at them. They may not always be able to quantify the nature or explain the focus of their hope, but it is very real and the results are usually quite remarkable. *This is certainly true of Christian hope.*

CHRISTIAN HOPE . . .

It is on the question of focus that Christian hope finds its unique characteristic. The focus of hope is always of significance and frequently determines the reality of such hope. The hope of some, for instance, is centred on personal health and they place great store upon their strength of body. For others, the power of their intellect or the extent of their material possessions is the determining factor in their hope for the future. Natural ability or their friendship with people of influence provides them with all the hope they feel they need.

## . . . Centred on God

The Christian hope is firmly placed and finds its central focus in God. In this regard it builds upon a foundation already laid in the Old Testament where there are clear indications that God was the focus of people's hope. Jeremiah the prophet, for instance, refers to God as 'the hope of Israel' – the one on whom the expectations of Israel rested, the one who would fulfil her longings. The author of Psalm 71 reinforces such belief when, in old age, he reflects upon his life. He comes to the conclusion that God has been his hope from the beginning – and will be to the end. 'You are my hope, Lord, since boyhood . . . my hope will never fade.'

Surrounded by the elaborate, meaningful and symbolic ritual of the religion of their day, Jeremiah, the psalmist and many others witness to the truth that their hope was focused primarily in God. The same is true today. Religion is a source of comfort and support to many people, myself included. It can help to maintain and deepen hope. But that hope, ultimately, is centred in God and not religion. Likewise faith is of vital importance to me and to millions of others, yet, at the end of the day, my hope as a Christian is not focused in my faith. Faith can wax and wane. Faith, as we saw in chapter 7, can sometimes be overwhelmed by the darkness of doubt and despair. It is the object of our faith, God alone, who is our ultimate hope.

The same can be said with regard to the Bible and the Church. The source of much of my daily inspiration as a Christian disciple so often comes to me through the words and truths of the Bible. Likewise the fellowship of the Christian Church and the loving sense of community which I share with other Christians are of immense value and importance to me on my journey through life. Both the Bible and the Church are God's gifts and I rejoice in them. But I know that more important than the Bible is the one of whom it speaks. And of greater lasting significance than the Church is the one whom the Church worships and serves.

God is the Alpha and the Omega. That is, he is the beginning and the end. He is the beginning and the end of religion, faith, the Bible and the Church. He and he alone is supreme as the centre and focus of hope for the Christian. In the end all these other things will be stripped away, but God remains. In the beginning God . . . and in the end God. The hymn-writer expressed it well when he wrote, 'All my hope on God is founded . . .'.

### . . . As revealed in Jesus Christ

The Christian hope which is centred on God is based supremely on the truth of God that is so clearly revealed in the life, death and resurrection of his Son, Jesus Christ. That truth, as displayed by Jesus, contains real hope not just for the so-called spiritually élite but for the whole world – and especially for those who might least expect it. Again and again in the stories and teaching of Jesus we are made aware of the fact that some rather surprised and surprising people will be included in the Kingdom of God. As Jesus said to some of the religious leaders of his day, 'In truth I tell you, tax collectors and prostitutes are making their way into the kingdom of God before you . . .

you did not believe . . . and yet the tax collectors and prostitutes did' (Matthew 21:31, 32).

It is a hope not based on an ethereal figure so far removed from us as to carry little relevance for us. It is good news of a hope which is based on the obedience, humility and vulnerability of Jesus. It is a hope based upon his powerlessness, upon his being scourged and derided, upon his being spat upon and reviled. It is a hope based upon his being judged and condemned, upon his being bound by others and led away to the outside, the periphery of the city. It is a hope based upon his being wounded and hurt and rejected and forsaken – upon his crying out and dying. *For this was the man God raised from the dead.* These were the conditions which were vanquished; these were the powers that could not destroy hope. There is therefore hope for all who share the experiences of Jesus, the humble, the powerless, the reviled, the marginalised, those who feel rejected and forsaken, the wounded, the hurt and the dying. The resurrection of Jesus Christ from the dead clearly declares that Christian hope is valid for the hopeless.

It is very significant that Peter, who seemed to be the acknowledged leader among the disciples of Jesus, saw the resurrection of Jesus as the great source of Christian hope. I say significant because when he first heard that Jesus intended to die to save the world Peter was very annoyed. Indeed he became quite belligerent and actually rebuked Jesus for suggesting such a thing. In fact he was so obsessed about telling Jesus how foolish he was to contemplate such a course of action, that he chose to ignore, or failed to hear, the promise of resurrection which accompanied it. The encounter makes fascinating reading:

From then onwards Jesus began to make clear to his disciples that he was destined to go to Jerusalem and suffer grievously at the hands of the elders and chief priests and scribes and to be put to death and to be raised up on the third day. Then, taking him aside, Peter started to rebuke him. 'Heaven preserve you, Lord', he said, 'this must not happen to you.' But he turned and said to Peter, 'Get behind me, Satan! You are an obstacle in my path, because you are thinking not as God thinks but as human beings do.'

Matthew 16:21–3

Peter was put firmly in his place but, and here is the truly significant thing, he learnt his lesson well. The penny actually dropped – as the letter attributed to him makes clear. The death of Jesus, far from being the disaster he had predicted, had become, along with the resurrection, the source of a vibrant and eternal hope:

Blessed be God the Father of our Lord Jesus Christ, who in his great mercy has given us a new birth into a living hope through the resurrection of Jesus Christ from the dead and into a heritage that can never be spoilt or soiled and never fade away. It is reserved in heaven for you who are being kept safe by God's power through faith until the salvation which has been pre-pared is revealed at the final point of time.

1 Peter 1:3–5

Peter clearly believed, and the Christian religion uni-versally declares, that because Jesus was raised from the dead Christians have a living hope – a hope which can never be diminished nor destroyed, nor will it ever dis-appear. It finds its base in the love of God which never comes to an end.

## A HOPE FOR ALL SEASONS . . .

As a young boy I remember being captivated by the mechanics of a weather vane which involved the figures of a woman wearing a summer dress and sun-glasses and a man wearing a raincoat and holding an umbrella. Of course, in those days feminism and male chauvinism had not yet become social issues! For hours I would watch the antics of those diminutive figures, hoping that the weather would change every few minutes so that I could see the two performers do their stuff. When the weather was fine, out would come the woman in her summer clothes and sun-glasses. When the weather was foul, out came the man in raincoat and brolly. When the weather was indeterminate they both hovered in the doorway – neither out nor in! My young mind couldn't immediately grasp why it was that the woman only appeared when the sun shone and the man only when it rained. The former seemed overworked in the summer, while the latter had to do overtime in the winter.

Christian hope is not so selective. It is a hope for all seasons.

For *winter* – when light and sunshine are in short supply. Those periods of life when suffering, depression and doubt threaten to overwhelm and crush us. But wasn't that the situation one Friday outside the gates of Jerusalem? Was there ever such a winter's day, when the very Light of the World seemed to be extinguished. Yet the force of evil could not destroy the power of love. The arms which were nailed to the cross stretched out to embrace the world in love; to welcome a dying man to paradise and to forgive those who were crucifying the Son of God. Jesus showed that hope can triumph in the experience of winter.

For *spring* – the season of rebirth and new life. Picasso's famous yet stark picture, *Guernica*, was painted when the town of that name was heavily bombed by Franco's fascist forces during the Spanish Civil War. Picasso was outraged and his enormous picture, painted in black, white and grey, is a painful, grotesque commentary on modern warfare. Everything in the picture is about death and destruction – except one small detail. Down at the bottom is a broken sword. It has a wooden handle and from the wood there is springing out a small twig and a bud – an act of defiance in the midst of so much destruction. It is a symbol of spring, of hope, of resurrection, of life irrepressibly breaking through the power of death.

For *summer* – when 'God is in his heaven and all is right with the world'. Those periods of life when prosperity, health and happiness envelop us and hope seems unnecessary and unimportant. Yet in the summer experiences of life the signs of hope are all around us and we need to recognise them and be thankful for them. We need to welcome those periods of well-being and the opportunity they present to grow in our understanding of God and his world. They provide us with space to develop deep roots of faith and love and rich reservoirs of hope in preparation for the storms of winter. It is a time for noticing the flower with the broken stem in the midst of a technicoloured garden – a time for bringing hope to those less fortunate than ourselves.

For *autumn* – the season of 'mist and mellow fruitfulness'. The so-called melancholy season of decay and decline, of ageing and preparing for death. Yet it is the most colourful season of all. A period of the year filled with the magnificent, swirling flames of yellow and red and orange. Symbolic, I believe, of the fact that Christian hope can transform a season of melancholy into a wonderful period of joy and adventure. For surely, 'the process of ageing, when suffused with trust in God's providential

care not only can be but must be an adventure.' Autumn
– the season of warm hope. Oh yes, the autumn leaves
fall to dust. But not before they have freely and gaily
danced in the wind!

### . . . And for all time

Because it is centred in the character of God, Christian
hope extends not only beyond all seasons but also beyond
all measurements of time and space for God is not bound
by such things. He is greater than his creation and he
refuses to abandon it. He fills the universe with his presence and he dwells with those who are humble in heart.
He is our Father, our God and the very ground of our
being. He is totally dependable, utterly trustworthy and
he is on our side. It is of immense and everlasting significance that even the heart-rending cry of dereliction from
the cross, 'My God, my God, why have you forsaken me?'
and the experience of desolation which it represented was
penetrated by hope. Listen to the final words from the
cross:

> It was now about the sixth hour and the sun's light
> failed, so that darkness came over the whole land until
> the ninth hour. The veil of the Sanctuary was torn right
> down the middle. Jesus cried out in a loud voice saying,
> 'Father, into your hands I commit my spirit.' With these
> words he breathed his last.
>
> Luke 23:44–6

He had felt abandoned by God, now he abandons himself
to God. Hope and trust triumph over fear and forsakenness. He places himself in the hands of God. The safest
place in all the world – and in all time – in which to be.

To be held in the hands of God is to be held in the love

of God and ultimately that is the true and only source of Christian hope. That is why Paul in his wonderful letter to the Christians at Rome spelt it out so clearly and in such unmistakeable terms:

> Can anything cut us off from the love of Christ – can hardships or distress, or persecution, or lack of food and clothing, or threats of violence . . . No; we come through all these things triumphantly victorious, by the power of him who loved us. For I am certain of this: neither death nor life, nor angels nor principalities, nothing already in existence and nothing still to come, nor any power, nor the heights nor the depths, nor any created thing whatever, will be able to come between us and the love of God, known to us in Christ Jesus our Lord.
>
> Romans 8:35–9

Nothing. Nothing. Nothing in all creation. Nothing in heaven or earth. Nothing in time, space or eternity can separate us from the love of God in Jesus Christ. Nothing. No wonder I rejoice to write and speak about the gospel, for the very word means *Good News*, and is there any news that can match that for goodness? It is that gospel which I commend to you.

## Questions

1. Why do you think so many people place their hope in transient things?
2. Is there a place for both optimism and pessimism in the Christian life or does hope automatically replace them?
3. How do you account for the quite remarkable examples

of enduring hope which are to be found in people who lay claim to no particular faith?

4. Must Christian hope be always thought of in terms of the future, i.e. 'Pie in the sky when you die'? Is there no practical application of hope for today's world and today's problems and uncertainties?

5. Consider a particularly difficult set of circumstances that you are aware of in the life of a friend, organisation or group. How would you bring hope into that situation?